Police Politics:
A Comparative Study
of Three Cities

Police Politics:
A Comparative Study of Three Cities

Leonard Ruchelman

Ballinger Publishing Company ● Cambridge, Mass.
A Subsidiary of J.B. Lippincott Company

363.2
R 82 p
95295
nov. 1975

Library of Congress Catalog Card Number: 73-17426

International Standard Book Number: 0-88410-206-8

Printed in the United States of America

Library of Congress Cataloging in Publication Data

Ruchelman, Leonard I
        Police politics.
        1. New York (City)—Police—Political activity. 2. Philadelphia—
Police—Political activity. 3. Chicago—Police—Political activity. I. Title.
HV8138.R8   363.2   73-17426
ISBN 0-88410-206-8

To Charles Michael

Contents

List of Figures and Tables

Figures

Tables

Preface

The purpose of this book is to develop a policy framework by which to better explain the role of the police bureaucracy in community affairs. Policemen, after all, are thinking, feeling human beings who act and react on the basis of changing societal conditions. That they should seek to assert themselves on questions of social policy comes as no surprise. But while it is generally recognized that the police have always been subject to forces in the political environment, the converse of this has been largely ignored in the existing literature: namely, how the police as a power bloc in its own right affects community politics.

     I should like to convey my gratitude to all those who helped me to achieve this objective, particularly Professor Joseph Logsdon who assisted in the initial discussions. Special thanks to my academic colleagues who read the manuscript and made comments. Special thanks also to Morton Schoolman who helped in the early stages of research and my wife Diana who offered valuable criticism and looked after matters of style.

Leonard Ruchelman
Lehigh University
Bethlehem, Penna.

Police Politics:
A Comparative Study
of Three Cities

Chapter One

Introduction: Political Dimensions of the Police Role

The involvement of police in community affairs is nothing new. When American cities were expanding in the nineteenth century, preserving the civic order was a matter of great concern. Newcomers from strange lands, rootless travelers, and the class and racial tensions of an evolving industrial order made cities frightening places for the established citizenry. The growing reliance on law enforcement called forth by these conditions contributed to delicate and often tense relations between the police and those others in the community who were subject to them or who wanted to dominate them. Major contenders in the police environment of most large cities usually included immigrant groups, politicians, city officials, reform organizations, labor groups, newspapers, and even the state legislatures. [1]

Particularly significant in this regard have been the political parties. In the not too distant past, police jobs and promotions were viewed by the leaders of the dominant party as part of their lawful spoils to be used for rewarding the faithful and punishing the opposition. Where the police also administered election procedures, battles for control of the force were especially intense. Similarly, members of the underworld have always had strong stakes in the quality of law enforcement. Though this had long been implicit in police work, the prohibition and depression days of the 1920's and 1930's demonstrated more than ever before how racketeers, gamblers, and traffickers in prostitution require tolerance and even support by the police if they are to prosper. [2]

In view of this, reform groups have long pressed for laws which would discourage police collusion with "outside" interests. Typical of such concerns was the report in 1931 of the National Commission on Law Observance and Law Enforcement, otherwise known as the Wickersham Commission (after its chairman). "The chief evil," it was argued, "lies in the insecure, short term of service of the chief or executive head of the police force and in his being subject

while in office to the control of politicians in the discharge of his duties." [3]
Significantly, among the "politicians" identified as the cause of poor law-
enforcement was the mayor of the city:

> The chief is usually appointed by the mayor. . . . Such appointment
> is, however, never a guaranty of competency for the place of the
> person appointed, but is simply an assurance that he is the personal
> appointee of the mayor and subject to his arbitrary control, or, more
> likely, that he is satisfactory to the party politicians whom the
> mayor felt obliged to consult before he dared risk confirmation of
> his nominee.[4]

Nor did the Commission seem to place any great faith in the workings of democracy:

> The theory that the mayor, representing the people, will exercise
> wisdom in conducting the business of the city and, being directly
> responsible to the electors, will do his utmost to protect lives
> and property of inhabitants and preserve the peace, has been badly
> shattered, judged by the caliber of police service which is to be
> found in the majority of the communities in this country.[5]

Following this analysis, the Commission proceeded to recommend
ways of "professionalizing" the whole police force: introducing civil service,
hiring better men and providing better training. Such prescription did not go
unheeded. Rules pertaining to recruitment, promotion, tenure, and compensa-
tion were gradually instituted in America's cities as the means of reducing the
influence of "outsiders"; and special training programs were introduced to assure
competence in job performance.

By the 1960's, however, the growing bureaucratization of police
personnel could be identified as the source of a new and unexpected development—it launched the police as an independent political force. Like other civil
servants, the police had formed associations by which they could better protect
and promote their own interests. Where permitted by law, such organizations
engage in negotiations with city hall on questions of working conditions. In addition, many of them lobby on the state and municipal levels for the purpose of
influencing personnel policy and salary scales. However, other techniques have
recently been tried as well: the "blue-flu" (i.e., calling in sick), picketing and the
slowdown have been effected in places like New York City, Detroit, Cleveland,
Boston, and Newark. Even more important, there is growing evidence that the
police bureaucracies are looking beyond the typical concerns of improving

material benefits and are seeking to assert themselves on vital questions of social policy. On such issues as the proper limits to civil protest and the rights of defendants in criminal proceedings, police are likely to see themselves as experts.

Though police militancy is in many ways similar to the militancy of other public employees, there are some important differences which pose considerably greater potential for the police as a political force. First, virtually all police organizations are essentially closed systems. Policemen must enter the force from the lowest rank, irrespective of previous experience, and work their way up through the organization. Contrary to most other forms of public and private employment, policemen usually cannot transfer to another police organization as a way of furthering their careers. Under such circumstances, pressures of conformity—the need to "get-along" and "go-along"—are substantial. [6]

Another factor pertains to the semimilitary form or organization which is pervasive in police work and the consequent stress on hierarchy and chain-of-command. Compared to other bureaucracies, there tends to be greater authority in the upper levels of the command structure. Thus, control over promotions and disciplinary action makes coercion possible, and pressure could be exerted on lower ranking members to work for a particular cause.

A third factor which bears on police power, actual or potential, is the fact that the police have a practical monopoly on the legal use of force in our society. Consequently, the growing politicization of the police poses a fundamental threat of coercion in community affairs. Persons who oppose the police could be intimidated with arrest or warnings of arrest.

RESEARCH APPROACH

The special dimensions of police politics vary from city to city. As communities differ in political style (loosely defined here as the way in which issues are resolved), so too will its police politics differ. The police, after all, are not immune to forces in the political environment and are subject to pressures and demands that emanate from elected officials, political executives, parties and interest groups.

However, the converse of this must also be considered: namely, the idea that police politics affects community politics. As a power bloc in its own right, the police have a stake in the political process. For example, they have an interest in the kinds of laws that are passed and whether these laws will be likely to restrict them in their jobs or give them wider latitude. Therefore, the research problem that we have defined is to assess the impact of police on the political environment. In this light, we try to discern patterns of political behavior among the police and to weigh the implications of this for the larger community. Matters which are essentially internal to the workings of the police bureaucracy are not considered, e.g., promotions, salaries, time schedules.

The basic approach is to investigate and compare important issues of police policy in three cities: New York City, Philadelphia, and Chicago. Covering the years 1966 to 1969, we focus on three overlapping policy areas which have received a great deal of attention in the news media of all three cities. They have been selected for study because of the way they demonstrate the changing political role of the police in society. However, this does not preclude the possibility that other issues may be equally revealing. The policy areas are as follows:

Civil Review and Accountability of the Police: This subject goes to the heart of any democratic system since it focuses on the question of civil watchfulness and control of the military arm of the community. A fundamental question here is who watches and commands the police and how the police respond.

The Law and Order Issue: This subject is complex because it has come to mean different things to different people. For the purposes of this study, we define it as the rights of the individual versus the obligation of the community to protect life and property. Decisions are observed in three types of situations: conditions of civil protest; conditions of civil disorder; conditions of due process, e.g., matters of bail, self-incrimination,legal counsel, search and seizure, cruel and unusual punishment.

Police-Community Relations: Here we are interested in the way the police are structured into the community. We account for decisions which determine how the police relate to other groups and participate in other jurisdictions, e.g., minority groups, education.

Methodology

This study concentrates primarily on the process by which issues are resolved rather than on a thorough treatment of the issues themselves. In each issue we attempt to discern the nature of participation which includes the point of view of key participants, power resources brought to bear, and the degree of success as measured by the outcome of an issue. Careful attention is directed to determining which individuals or agencies "most often initiated the proposals that were finally adopted or most often successfully vetoed the proposal of others." [7] (In a few cases a particular decision is judged applicable to more than one issue and is therefore considered more than once.) We ask, for example, was the mayor successful, on what kinds and how many proposals, why, and if not, why not? Furthermore, the pursuit of such questions in three cities rather than one affords opportunity for more enriched insights; for a comparative focus permits inquiry into why certain patterns are revealed in some places or situations but not in others—e.g., why is the mayor successful in city A but not in city B?

While there were many decision-making cases, we consider only those that were of community-wide significance. Cases that were essentially parochial (e.g., limited to a few individuals) or temporary in nature (e.g., experimental programs) are excluded. Furthermore, we focus on decision making as an aspect of open conflict. Important as it may be, we do not purport to generalize about the more covert qualities of power.[8] Data was derived from the newspapers of the three cities, relevant documents and studies, as well as interviews.[9]

Before proceeding to the data, we should take cognizance of some other difficulties which are inherent in our methodology. For one, political confrontations can result in mixed outcomes thereby making it difficult to assess success or failure. In the few cases where this did appear as a problem, we relied on the assessments of observors who could judge outcomes in light of the surrounding circumstances. Secondly, where more than one participant seemed to share in an outcome and where fine distinctions could not be made, we attributed multiple scores. Because of the controversial nature of our subject matter, however, and the publicity and discussions which naturally follow controversy, coding was not as difficult as might ordinarily be supposed.

Community Power Structure Analysis

An underlying interest of community research is to treat the important question of "who governs". Since the 1950's and the writings of C. Wright Mills [10] and Floyd Hunter,[11] social scientists have been engaged in debate over concepts and methods which could best answer this question. Whether communities are essentially elitist (run by a few persons who have a monopoly of power resources) or pluralist (run by competing elites) has been a fundamental part of this debate. Floyd Hunter has been one of the chief proponents of the former and Robert Dahl has proposed the latter.[12] A third group of scholars who have been labeled "neo-elitist" contends that while communities tend to be organized for the benefit of the few, prevailing community biases and "nondecision making", i.e., decisions not to make decisions on important questions, are especially crucial.[13]

The present work draws from these earlier efforts. But rather than designing a study which purports to generalize about the overall political life of a city as Hunter does in Atlanta and Dahl does in New Haven, we deliberately take a different route: We focus instead on one policy area in three communities. The expected pay-off is greater accuracy of findings and more controlled generalizations. Moreover, so long as the questions raised are important enough, (for example, questions which pertain to the efficacy and viability of democracy in America's cities) justification for such conceptualization speaks for itself.

By way of proceeding, Chapter 2 lays the groundwork by describing the police setting in New York, Philadelphia and Chicago. This includes discussion of the basic environmental characteristics of these cities, their political and governmental structure, and special qualities of law enforcement organization. The next three chapters consider key police issues in the areas of civil review and accountability, law and order, and police-community relations. An overview of patterns of police politics and how they effect the outer parameters of city politics is presented in the last chapter.

NOTES

1. For the history of this in New York and Boston see James F. Richardson, *The New York Police: Colonial Times to 1901* (New York: Oxford University Press, 1970); and Robert Lane, *Policing the City: Boston 1822-1885* (Cambridge, Mass.: Harvard University Press, 1967).
2. The significance of this in contemporary times is analyzed by John A. Gardner, *The Politics of Corruption* (New York: Russell Sage Foundation, 1970); also the President's Commission on Law Enforcement and Administration of Justice, *Task Force Report: The Police* (Washington, D.C.: U.S. Government Printing Office, 1967), chap. 7.
3. The National Commission on Law Observance and Enforcement, *Report on the Police* (Washington, D.C.: U.S. Government Printing Office, 1931), p. 1.
4. *Ibid.*, p. 2.
5. *Ibid.*, p. 49.
6. On this matter, see the President's Commission on Law Enforcement and Administration of Justice, *The Challenge of Crime in a Free Society* (New York: Avon Books, 1968), pp. 283, 284.
7. Robert Dahl. *Who Governs?* (New Haven: Yale University Press, 1961), p. 124. Our method of looking at decisions is essentially similar to Dahl's except that we study one major policy area, i.e., the police area, rather than three different ones and we compare three cities instead of observing one. See Appendix B. Section V, *ibid.*, pp. 332-334.
8. See the article by Peter Bachrach and Morton S. Baratz which is critical of Robert Dahl's methods. "Two Faces of Power," *The American Political Science Review*, LVI (December, 1962), 947-52.
9. The interview method posed some very real difficulties in our three sample cities because of resistance and suspicion by those most directly involved in police affairs.

10. See particularly, C. Wright Mills, *The Power Elite* (New York: Oxford University Press, 1956).
11. Floyd Hunter, *Community Power Structure* (Chapel Hill: University of North Carolina Press, 1952).
12. Robert Dahl, *op. cit.*
13. Peter Bachrach and Morton S. Baratz, *Power and Poverty* (New York: Oxford University Press, 1970).

Chapter Two

The Police Setting: New York, Philadelphia, Chicago

The selection of New York City, Chicago and Philadelphia for investigation is basically a choice of convenience. Nevertheless, ranking first, second and fourth among the largest metropolitan centers in the nation, they evidence a history of what we have defined as police politics and especially a preoccupation with civilian review board and "law and order" issues. Such concerns, we should note, grow out of environmental conditions and particularly what has come to be recognized as urban crisis conditions; namely, high crime rates and civil disorder. The statistics in Table 2-1 give a general picture of this.

A related dimension concerns race relations in all three cities. As the number of blacks has increased, tensions with the older population groups have grown. Here is the basis to much of the present day discussion about lawlessness in America. Various surveys show that when city officials discuss rioting or the escalating crime rate, they are talking, for the most part, about those areas in the central city which contain large concentrations of poor blacks which the police try to contain.[1] Table 2-2 gives us some basic statistics which illustrate the changing distribution of black populations over the last decade in New York City, Philadelphia and Chicago.

Before we analyze these trends as they pertain to police politics, however, it would be useful to focus on the formal police organizations of our three sample cities and their political surroundings. The basic interest here is to account for those political and administrative arrangements which serve as background to the analysis which follows in the succeeding chapters. Other less formal components of the police setting such as the roles of leading personalities, interest groups and party organizations will receive careful treatment in other sections of the book as part of our data.

Table 2-1.   Law Enforcement Profile of Three Cities by Selected Characteristics

Civil disorders—intensity index of more than 5 (January, 1967–August, 1968)*	Date civil disturbance began	Length of disturbance in days	Number arrested, injured, killed	National Guard called	Intensity index*
Chicago**	5/12/67	1	37–12–0	no	8
	7/26/67	2	80–0–0	no	11
	2/27/68	1	49–0–0	no	6
	4/4/68	8	2931–500–9	yes	457
	7/25/68	1	3–12–0	no	5
Philadelphia	1/20/68	1	7–11–0	no	5
	4/4/68	7	100–37–0	no	28
New York City	7/23/67	3	47–150–2	no	54
	7/29/67	3	76–58–0	no	28
	9/4/67	5	76–58–1	no	31
	4/5/68	2	400–0–0	no	42
	4/9/68	2	515–97–1	no	83
	4/23/68	4	1000–231–0	no	173
Crime rate per 100,000 inhabitants	1966	1967		1968	1969
Chicago	3012.0	3244.6		3334.4	3627.9
Philadelphia	1490.8	1472.8		1638.4	1823.5
New York City	4059.1	4850.2		5983.0	5867.9
Number of police officers	1966	1967		1968	1969
Chicago	11,113	11,428		12,006	12,205
Philadelphia	7,234	7,393		7,319	7,439
New York City	27,418	27,462		29,939	31,578

Source: J. Robert Havlick and Mary K. Wade, "The American City and Civil Disorders," *Urban Data Service* (Washington, D.C.: International City Managers' Association, 1969); Federal Bureau of Investigation, *Uniform Crime Reports*, 1966–1969 (Washington, D.C.: U.S. Department of Justice); U.S. Bureau of the Census.

*According to the scheme of Havlick and Wade, *ibid.*, the intensity index is determined in the following way: 10 points for each day of disturbance; 1 point for each arrest; 3 points for each injury; 5 points for each death; 10 points if the national guard was called.

**Figures for Chicago do not include the results of the disorders during the Democratic National Convention.

Table 2-2.   Percent Black Population in Three Cities, 1960 and 1970.

	Total population, 1970	*1960*	*1970*
Philadelphia	1,950,098	26%	34%
Chicago	3,369,359	23%	33%
New York City	7,895,563	14%	21%

Source: U.S. Bureau of the Census

New York City

Whether viewed from the criteria of size, heterogeneity of interests, or institutional complexity, most observors seem to agree that New York City affairs are more intricate if not more confusing than those of any other large city. Barry Gottehrer, for many years a high ranking assistant to Mayor Lindsay, comments on the governmental aspect: "The administrative machinery of the city has become so complicated and bureaucratic that few people know how their government functions. . . . As a result, the city government has grown farther and farther away from its citizens, smug and indecisive after years of one-party (Democratic) rule." [2] Professor David Rodgers, a long-time student of New York City, confirms this assessment: [3]

> The city has developed . . . as a large planless hodgepodge, where the decisions affecting its physical layout are made mainly by large economic interests (developers, contractors, banks, insurance companies). Its politics generally are played as a kind of brokerage game where all groups can defend private interests against an unstated, undefined, or weakly defined social goal. Mayor Lindsay has been trying to reverse that process, but the power of established interests and institutions is difficult to overcome.

There are a number of reasons for this state of affairs. As provided by the City Charter, the Mayor must deal with two legislative bodies in the course of making public policy: the City Council with thirty-five representatives and the Board of Estimate which is composed of the Mayor, the Council President, the Controller, and five Borough Presidents. All are elected at the same time for four year terms. Basic to the structure of New York City government, moreover, is the fact that it subsumes five counties, each one of which is a center of power in its own right: each has a Borough President who serves on the Board of Estimate, each has two councilmen elected at large, each has its own county offices, and each has its own party organization (there being no city-wide party).

In addition to this formal governmental fragmentation, there is growing factionalism within the city's party organizations. Both the Democratic and

Republican parties have been subject to the divisive effects of intraparty squabbling between "regulars" and "reformers," professionals and amateurs. Tammany Hall, New York City's notorious political machine, exists no more. It was of no great surprise, then, when Republican reform candidate John Lindsay, running on a ticket which included Democrats and Liberals, won the mayoralty election of 1965. Lindsay won the mayoralty a second time in 1969, but this time as the candidate of the Liberal party, and with only 43 percent of the popular vote. And in 1971, because of disgruntlement with the Nixon administration, he became a Democrat. Here is the basis to much of the Lindsay regime's impotence. Lacking a permanent party organization which could tie together the various political sectors of the city, the Mayor has tended to become isolated within his own office.

Indeed, if we look at one very crucial area, relations with public employees, we find that Lindsay's efforts have not been very effective. From the very first day when transport workers began a thirteen day walkout, John V. Lindsay's reign has been clouded by crises. This was followed at intervals by striking school teachers, garbage collectors, drawbridge operators and even policemen. In this light, a key question in New York City is: can the Mayor control and direct the public bureaucracy?

In the police jurisdiction, the City Charter of 1961 gives the Mayor some important tools. He has the authority to appoint the Police Commissioner for a term of five years unless he decides to remove him sooner. More generally, the Charter recognizes the Mayor as "the chief executive officer of the city" and gives him broad budgetary powers. His immediate staff in the Executive Office (which includes the Budget Director) and two Deputy Mayors assist him in supervising and coordinating the police with the other city agencies (e.g., Fire, Sanitation, Correction, Traffic, Parks and Recreation, Human Resources).

Along with the Mayor and other city administrators, the Police Commissioner cannot avoid the effects of political fragmentation. In the performance of his law enforcement duties, for example, he must be prepared to deal with five different county District Attorneys and five separate county court systems in addition to the city law enforcement authorities (e.g., the city courts, the Commissioner of Investigation). On questions of political support, it is not necessarily the case that he can depend on the Mayor's constituency base.

What makes the Commissioner's job even more complex are various autonomous and semiautonomous public bodies which have direct bearing on police affairs. This includes the Civil Service Commission which regulates police recruitment and promotions up to the post of captain. Such other agencies as the Housing Authority, the New York Port Authority and the Metropolitan

Transportation Authority have their own police which require coordination with the city police.

In their assessment of the Police Commissioner's role, Wallace Sayre and Herbert Kaufman observe that the ". . . basic conditions of his leadership and initiative are rarely fully mastered by the Police Commissioner. Resolute outsiders and insiders, in their turn as Commissioners, have each expended great energies and varied strategies upon this dilemma without triumphant results." [4] The fairly high rate of turnover of Commissioners during the 1960's would seem to lend some credence to this statement. When Michael J. Murphy resigned toward the end of Mayor Robert Wagner's Democratic administration, a number of successors followed: Vincent Broderick lasted for little more than a year when Mayor Lindsay replaced him in 1966 with Howard R. Leary who had been the Police Commissioner of Philadelphia; Leary resigned in 1970 and Lindsay then appointed Patrick V. Murphy who had been the Police Commissioner of Detroit. Overall, a total of four Commissioners were rotated over a six-year period.

The Department which the Police Commissioner heads is one of the largest of the city's agencies. But more than the factor of size, is the variety of Departmental powers and responsibilities which make the Commissioner's job an especially difficult one. From the Charter alone, the Department is authorized to "preserve the public peace, prevent crime. . . . suppress riots, mobs and insurrections, . . . protect the rights of persons and property, guard the public health, preserve order at elections and all public meetings and assemblages. . . ." [5] It also has powers of general supervision and inspection over pawnbrokers, vendors, dealers in junk and in secondhand merchandise and auctioneers within the city. But the greater part of the Department's duties are derived from state laws and local ordinances and codes too numerous to mention. All of these sources together, we should note, structure a service role as well as a watchdog role—i.e., the expectation that police patrols should provide assistance to people as well as protection.

The organizational means of administering such functions is illustrated in Figure 2-1. In the top command post sits the Commissioner who, according to the Charter, "shall have cognizance and control of the government, administration, disposition and discipline of the department, and control of the police force of the department." [6] Whether this formal provision of authority is sufficient to the leadership needs of the Commissioner is a matter to be explored later in the book. Seven Deputy Commissioners provide him with specialized staff assistance. The Charter states that the Commissioner can appoint them and remove them at his pleasure.

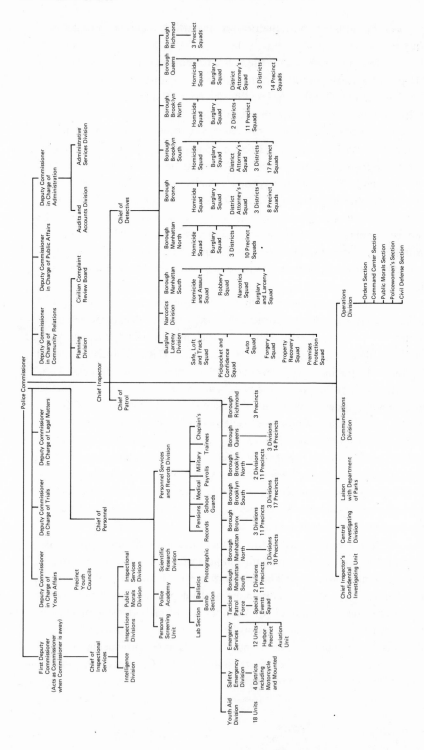

Figure 2-1. Organization, New York City Police Department

For practical purposes, the six most influential positions in the Department under the Commissioner are the First Deputy Commissioner, the Chief Inspector (who holds the highest ranking uniformed post), the Chief of Patrol (who commands more than 60 percent of the uniformed force), the Chief of Detectives, the Chief of Inspectional Services and the Chief of Personnel. As reflected in the organizational chart, six of the seven Deputy Commissioners—all but the First Deputy Commissioner—are considered less influential. Because their duties are more specialized, they are outside the line of command leading to the men who perform police work.

If the uniformed policemen are expected to abide by the commands which flow through the formal organizational channels of the Department, it is also the case that most of them are subject to the cues and directives of another overlapping organization—the Patrolmen's Benevolent Association. Founded in 1898 as a professional police organization, the P.B.A. has since grown to where its membership now includes over 95 percent of New York City's policemen. According to its constitution, the P.B.A. is the bargaining agent for "all the patrolmen of the City of New York in matters of policy, salaries, hours of employment and all other matters relating to the general welfare of its members."

Philadelphia

In contrast to most other large cities where the Democrats have been dominant, Republican party control of Philadelphia's politics lasted well into the twentieth century, even overcoming the national sweep of Franklin D. Roosevelt's New Deal during the 1930's and 1940's. By 1951, however, the Republican hegemony came to an end and the Democrats finally took charge under a new urban coalition of business, civic and professional groups. The two men most instrumental in achieving this were Joseph Clark, who was elected Mayor in 1951, and Richardson Dilworth, Clark's successor in the mayoralty. Both had Main-Line, Republican backgrounds and both were reformers.[7]

An important event at the time of this transition was the adoption of a new home-rule charter for Philadelphia which established a strong-mayor system of government. The Mayor was ultimately made "responsible for the conduct of the executive and administrative work of the City and for law-enforcement within its boundaries."[8] In addition, he was given strong powers over finance. He submits budget requests for all public agencies to the city council and during the fiscal year may reduce council appropriations for any department in order to avoid a deficit. Helping the Mayor direct the major administrative departments are four staff aids: a managing director who, with the mayor's consent, appoints and supervises the heads of the ten service departments including the police department; a director of finance who is in charge of accounting and the preparation of the operating budget; a city solicitor who is the legal adviser; and a city representative who make public appearances in behalf of the mayor.

The Charter, however, also confronts the Mayor with some important limitations. While he can use powers of appointment and removal to control the bureaucracy, he is limited in his influence by one of the most comprehensive merit systems of any city; as it works out, only about 200 appointive jobs are available to the mayor as patronage out of a total of 33,000 persons employed by the city. Furthermore, he is restricted to no more than two successive four year terms in office. While the Mayor's office is directly in command of the Police Department (the Mayor actually appoints the Commissioner and can remove him), there are other city offices which play a role in police affairs. Of particular significance is the District Attorney's office which does investigational work in liaison with the Police Department and on its own through the work of county detectives (a subdivision of the District Attorney's office). Philadelphia also has an elected Sheriff whose chief function is to carry out directives of the city's courts, i.e., warrants, writs, subpoenas. There is, in addition, an independent Civil Service Commission which administers the merit system up to the highest ranks excluding Deputy Commissioners.

Because of its legislative powers, the City Council must be acknowledged as another contender in the police setting. It is elected at the same time as the Mayor, every four years. Of its seventeen members, ten are elected from each of the council districts and seven are elected from the city–at–large. Of the latter seven positions, each party can nominate only five persons in order to assure some minority party representation.

Administrative direction, command and review of the Police Department is the Commissioner's responsibility. He is assisted in his duties by his immediate staff and two Deputy Commissioners. According to the City Charter, the Department functions to "preserve the public peace, prevent and detect crime, police the streets and highways and enforce traffic statutes, ordinances and regulations relating thereto." [9] It is also charged with enforcement of the statutes of the state of Pennsylvania and the ordinances of the city of Philadelphia. Figure 2–2 gives some idea of how the Department is organized to perform these functions. The majority of sworn personnel are, of course, found in the Uniform Forces; close to sixty percent are found in the patrol bureau alone.

During the period 1960 to 1970 there have been a total of four different commissioners in the city: Albert N. Brown resigned for reasons of health in 1963; Howard R. Leary resigned in 1966 to become police commissioner in New York City; Edward J. Bell resigned for reasons of health in 1967; and Frank Rizzo resigned in 1970 to run successfully for Mayor of Philadelphia. We should note that this high rate of turnover among commissioners took place during the administration of Mayor James H. Tate, the man who succeeded Richardson Dilworth in 1962.

If the turnover of Police Commissioners in Philadelphia has been high, this is not the case for the leadership of the Fraternal Order of the Police, Lodge 5. President Michael Harrington held on to his position from 1964 to 1972 when he was deposed by Charles Gallagher. It is estimated that more than ninety-nine percent of all Philadelphia policemen belong to the FOP. Besides providing a vehicle for comradeship among policemen, the organization negotiates with the city on working conditions, salaries and provides legal defense for any of its members who face either litigation or disciplinary action resulting from official job performance. We should also note that in contrast to the Patrolmen's Benevolent Association in New York City which has an essentially local orientation, the Fraternal Order of the Police is a national organization with its membership broken down into local lodges across the country. National headquarters is in Philadelphia.

Chicago

The key to understanding Chicago politics requires distinguishing between the city's formal governmental structure and its informal political structure. Edward C. Banfield, a long-time observor of Chicago, contends that from a purely formal perspective, the City has such a plethora of governing offices and bodies that it can hardly be said to have a government at all.[10] In addition to the city government, other public sovereignties in the Chicago area are the Board of Education, the Board of Trustees of the Sanitary District, the Chicago Park District, the Board of Commissioners of Cook County and the Forest Preserve District of Cook County. Each has its own taxing powers and officers who are either independently elected or, if appointed by the Mayor, are virtually independent of him.

A more detailed view of the formal governmental structure reveals a mayoralty office which is weaker than the ones in either New York or Philadelphia.[11] The Mayor shares executive authority with the City Treasurer and the City Clerk; all are elected at the same time for four-year terms. The City Council consists of the Mayor and fifty aldermen each of whom is elected from a ward on a nonpartisan basis. The Mayor presides over the Council, makes recommendations, and exercises a veto. The various departments and boards in the administrative sector are more directly accountable to the City Council than to the Mayor.

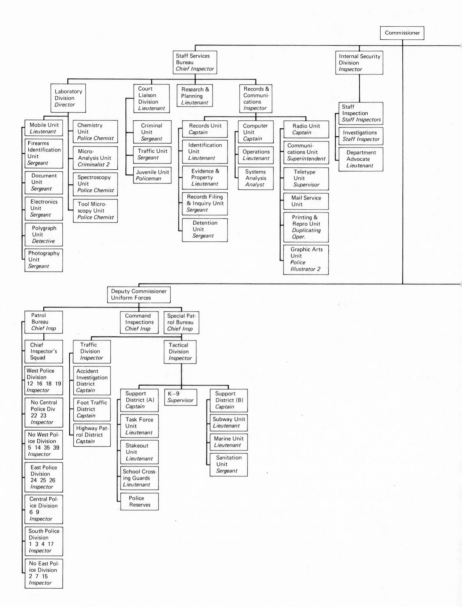

Figure 2-2. Organization, Philadelphia Police Department

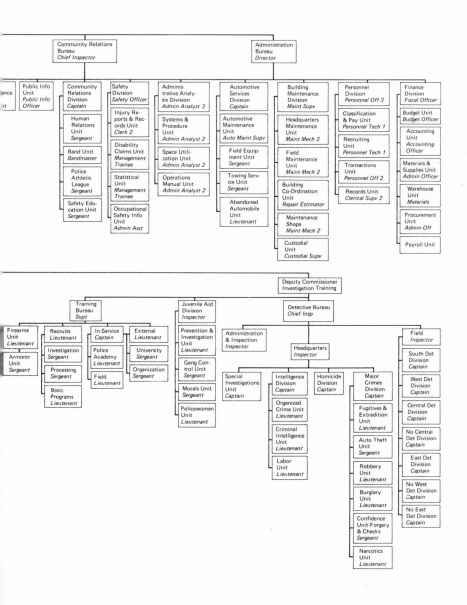

Because Chicago is located within Cook County—this is in contrast to Philadelphia which has absorbed Philadelphia County and New York City which subsumes five counties—county government has a far-reaching impact on the affairs of the City. Prominent in this regard are the President of the County Board, the Sheriff, the Coroner, the County Clerk, the State's Attorney and the County Treasurer. In addition, there is the County Board whose fifteen members make legislative policy.

In light of the diffuseness of governmental authority, a logical question is: How is Chicago managed? By and large, the major mechanism is the old-fashioned party machine as mastered by incumbent Mayor Richard J. Daley. Unlike New York City or Philadelphia, the reform movement of Chicago has remained weak and ineffective.[12] In his overlapping roles as mayor and chairman of the Cook County Democratic Committee, Daley has the means of controlling approximately three-fourths of the City Council members, the School Board, the Park Board, two-thirds of the County Board and many suburban offices. With surprising frequency, moreover, Daley's influence extends to the other county officers, the Governor and a majority bloc of state legislators.

Having been elected to the City's highest office for five consecutive four-year terms, Daley and his organization has functioned with virtually no effective opposition. It is estimated that he disposes of between 30,000 and 35,000 jobs, including county and city jobs, not to mention the jobs available to him through industry. Aided by an army of public employees, and in firm control of the policy-making machinery of government, Daley has succeeded in obligating everyone, citizens, labor, businessmen, and party workers alike, to his organization. Banfield and Wilson describe Chicago as a city "in which an extreme decentralization of authority has been overcome by an extreme centralization of power, the power being based on specific inducements."[13]

Accordingly, the operation of the Chicago Police Department is a reflection of both the centralizing and decentralizing aspects of the city's politics. The Municipal Code identifies "an executive department of the municipal government of the city which shall be known as the department of police. . . ." It further specifies that a Police Board of five members is to be appointed by the Mayor "by and with the consent of the City Council." The prime function of the Board is to suggest three persons for the position of Superintendent of Police, one of whom is then appointed by the Mayor. The Superintendent is to "serve at the pleasure of the mayor" and "shall be responsible for the general management and control of the police department, and shall have full and complete authority to administer the department in a manner consistent with the ordinances of the city, the laws of the State, and the rule and regulations of the police department."[14]

In addition to the Police Board, several other features weaken the Mayor's formal authority in police affairs. The Civil Service Board controls procedures for hiring and firing all police personnel through the rank of captain. The State's Attorney, who prosecutes all persons arrested by the police for everything but city ordinances, is an elected county officer and therefore responsible to another government unit. Other county officers who play a role in city law enforcement are the Sheriff and the Coroner. Under such circumstances of fragmented control, the police can often exercise their own judgment in the implementation of law enforcement policy—i.e., what laws are to be enforced and to what degree.

On occasion, police abuse in Chicago gets out of hand and when reported by the press, the Mayor must act to restore public confidence. This was the case in 1960 when the State's Attorney, a Republican, investigated a Chicago burglary ring and discovered that a number of city policemen were involved. The embarrassment of such scandal compelled Mayor Daley to impanel a blue-ribbon committee to recruit a new administrator who could reestablish the credibility of the police. The person finally selected for the new position of Superintendent of Police was Orlando W. Wilson, the dean of the school of criminology at the University of California at Berkeley. (Prior to 1960, the head of the Department held the title of Commissioner.) During his seven-year tenure, Wilson installed a new two million dollar communications system, consolidated police districts and generally upgraded police procedures. In 1967 he resigned and was replaced by James B. Conlisk, Jr., an old-timer in the Department.

Figure 2-3 shows the Chicago Police Department as it is presently organized. As can be seen, assisting the Superintendent are five Deputy Superintendents, one of which is designated First Deputy Superintendent. The latter serves as the Acting Superintendent in the absence of the Superintendent. As head of the Bureau of Operational Services, moreover, he commands the bulk of all police personnel. The five deputies together are, in essence, the structural frame around which all police activities flow.

Most of Chicago's policemen belong to three different organizations for the purpose of improving working conditions and raising salaries. The largest is the Confederation of Police (C.O.P.) with a total membership of seven thousand as of 1970. The Fraternal Order of Police (F.O.P.) has forty-seven hundred members and the Chicago Patrolmen's Association (C.P.A.), which began in 1916 and is the oldest, has four-thousand members. With considerable difficulty, the groups have tried to cooperate under the auspices of a joint council, but the results so far have been poor. Of further interest is the fact that the Police Department officially does not recognize the existence of these organizations.

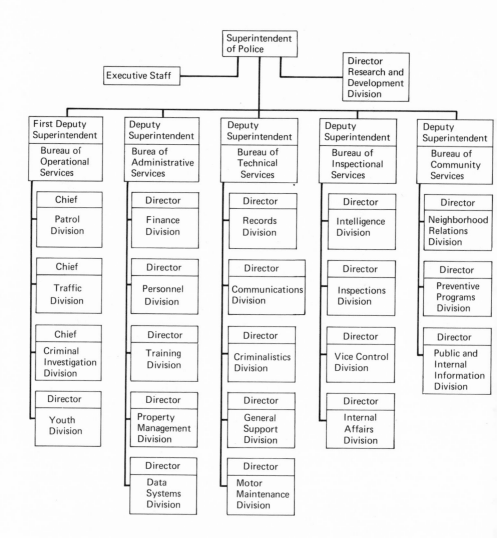

Figure 2-3.   Organization, Chicago Police Department

The State and Federal Role

Though the present study focuses on police politics within three cities, we must recognize that external sources, and particularly state and federal government, are an important part of the total police environment.

State government has always played a role in local law enforcement. Toward the latter part of the nineteenth century, state lawmakers often assumed major responsibility for structuring police operations. In 1857, for example, the New York legislature passed the so-called Metropolitan police bill which consolidated the police districts of the cities of New York and Brooklyn and the Counties of Kings, Westchester, and Richmond under a board of five commissioners appointed by the governor; for a number of years thereafter the state continued to direct the policing of the entire area. This precedent of establishing strong state control over local police was soon emulated throughout the United States and in certain cities in Missouri, Maryland, Massachusetts, and New Hampshire, it continues to exist.

What is more important in terms of contemporary concerns, is the fact that it is the state policy making bodies which still set much of the agenda for what the police are expected to do—i.e., enforcement of state laws which regulate the health, welfare, safety, and morals of the people; and, to a large extent, the state courts sit in judgment of such activities. Furthermore, in spite of "home rule" guarantees which assure powers of local self-government, the state capitals can still regulate the provision of basic police needs, e.g., rates of pay, pensions, hours of work, collective bargaining.

At the farther corners of the police setting are units of the federal government: courts, congressional committees, administrative agencies, U.S. attorneys. All of these are capable of intervening in the law enforcement affairs of local communities. Sometimes, as we shall see, such action meets with dramatic consequences. Mirroring the rising anxieties of the American people over "law and order," Congress enacted new legislation on crime and law enforcement during the 1960's. Most comprehensive was the Omnibus Crime Control and Safe Streets Act of 1968 which provided federal funds to states for projects designed to improve state and local law enforcement efforts. Under President Richard Nixon's urgings, Congress also enacted a number of stringent measures which bear directly on Bill of Rights guarantees. The District of Columbia Court Reform and Criminal Procedure Act of 1970, for example, contains highly controversial "no-knock" and "preventive detention" provisions. Another law is the Organized Crime Control Act of 1970 which permits an expanded use of evidence acquired by wire-tapping in dealing with racketeers.

Of additional significance in weighing the federal role have been a series of recent Supreme Court decisions on police practices. In such cases as

Mapp v. Ohio (1961), *Escobedo v. Illinois* (1964), *Miranda v. Arizona,* (1966), and *U.S. v. Wade* (1967), the Court has mandated that the due process guarantee of the 14th Amendment binds state and local policemen, as well as federal officers, to obey the various procedures established by the Bill of Rights. Consequently, on such matters as interrogation of suspects, seizure of evidence, electronic eaves dropping, and lineup procedures, the police of America's cities must now tread carefully. That the police have been unhappy with the Supreme Court and particularly the "Warren Court" (after Chief Justice Earl Warren who served from 1952 to 1969) is clear.[15] What they do about it is one of our interests in viewing the police politics of New York, Philadelphia and Chicago.

NOTES

1. See, for example, Angus Campbell, *White Attitudes Toward Black People* (Ann Arbor, Michigan: Institute for Social Research, 1971); Gary T. Marx, *Protest and Prejudice* (New York: Harper and Row, 1967); Joel D. Aberbach and Jack L. Walker, *Race in the City* (Boston: Little, Brown and Company, 1973).
2. Barry Gottehrer and the staff of the *New York Herald Tribune, New York City in Crisis* (New York: Pocket Books, 1965) p. 2.
3. David Rogers, *The Management of Big Cities* (Beverly Hills; Sage Publications, 1971), p. 26.
4. Wallace S. Sayre and Herbert Kaufman, *Governing New York City* (New York: W.W. Norton and Company, 1965), p. 287.
5. *New York City Charter* (New York: The City Record, Adopted November 7, 1961), Chapter 18, sec. 435.
6. *Ibid.,* chapter 18, sec. 434.
7. For an interesting analysis of the effects of the Clark and Dilworth leadership, see James Reichly, *The Art of Government* (New York: The Fund for the Republic, 1959).
8. *Philadelphia Home Rule Charter* (Adopted April 17, 1951), Article IV, Sec. 4–100.
9. *Ibid.,* Article V, Sec. 5–200.
10. Edward C. Banfield, *Political Influence* (New York: The Free Press, 1961), chap. 8.
11. Rather than a charter, it is Illinois state law and the Municipal Code which structures Chicago's government.
12. For an analysis of this, see James Q. Wilson, *The Amateur Democrat* (Chicago: The University of Chicago Press, 1962), chap. 3.
13. Edward C. Banfield and James Q. Wilson, *City Politics* (Cambridge, Mass.: Harvard University Press, 1963), p. 104.
14. *Municipal Code,* chap. 11, sec. 1–3, 5–6 (1968).
15. It is by no means likely that the more conservative "Burger Court" appointed by President Nixon will reverse many or most of the Warren Court

precedents in criminal procedure. See Howard Whitcomb, "Constitutional Revolution in Criminal Procedure," in *Who Rules the Police?* (New York: New York University Press, 1973), pp. 100–114, edited by Leonard Ruchelman.

Chapter Three

Civil Review and Accountability of the Police

Civil review and accountability of the police is analagous to the American principle of civilian control of the military. But while tradition and the United States Constitution clearly support the President as "Commander-in-Chief of the Army and Navy," the idea of external control of the police on the community level is fraught with ambiguity. The diffuseness of the political setting plus the vulnerability of elected officials to charges of "political interference" are what make this matter so complex.

One way of approaching the subject is to ask: How much civil review and how much accountability are present in our three sample cities? In this way we try to assess the extent to which civil authority is able to assert itself on questions of review and command and the ways in which the police respond. A related interest is to identify the arguments and competing proposals by which such matters are decided.

CIVIL REVIEW

As a measure of public watchfulness, we first inquire into the number and kinds of reviews which have taken place in each of our subject cities during the period 1966 to 1969, and whether they were initiated by forces external or internal to the city. (Reviews which do not affect the police force as a whole or which do not have some broad community significance are not included in our data.) The procedures referred to here are hearings, studies, and investigations undertaken by both public and private agencies or persons which are intended to have some important impact on public control of police activities. Indeed, as we shall see, grand juries, "blue-ribbon" committees, and special task force study groups can sometimes intervene dramatically in the law enforcement affairs

27

Table 3-1.   Civil Review of Police Activity: Investigations, Studies, Inquiries

	New York City	Philadelphia	Chicago
Number of reviews	12	8	12
Number of reviews initiated by forces external to the city	2	3	8
Number of reviews essentially critical of police and/or recommends limitations	8(1 external*) (7 internal**)	5(3 external*) (2 internal**)	8(7 external*) (1 internal**)

*This refers to the number of reviews initiated by forces external to the city.
**This refers to the number of reviews initiated by forces internal to the city.

of communities. Where effectively done, such endeavor can lead to reform of established police practices.

The findings in Table 3-1 provide us with a rough profile of this in New York City, Philadelphia and Chicago. In viewing the data, we should note that Table 3-1 not only distinguishes between reviews that originated inside and outside the city, but it also indicates the number of reviews which were essentially critical of police action or which recommended limitations on police behavior. The significance of this distinction is especially evident in the city of Chicago which we consider first.

Chicago

More than is the case for most American cities, the history of Chicago in the 1960's is a recounting of racial conflict, public protest and violence. Prominent during this time were black ghetto disturbances in 1966 and 1968, the confrontation of demonstrators and police during the Democratic National Convention of August, 1968, and the slaying by police of two Black Panther leaders in December of 1969. It is against this background of simmering unrest and forceful reaction that a series of investigations were initiated by various authorities to find out what had gone wrong and whether law enforcement had been effective.

Of some significance is the fact that seven reviews which originated outside of Chicago were the only essentially critical assessments made during the entire four year period under study. The one noncritical outside review, however, a Cook County Coroner's jury investigation of the police raid on Black Panther headquarters, was within the orbit of Mayor Daley's Democratic organization. But what lends special meaning to these findings is the way they contrast with internally sponsored inquiries: three out of the full total of four were essentially supportive or protective of police action, and the fourth merely recommended new police procedures during riots. (See Appendix C for a complete listing of reviews.)

When viewed overall, the review function appears to represent an obvious form of political sparring. This can be illustrated by the way the city has approached the problem of racial conflict in its slum areas. Compelled to respond to mounting civil rights demonstrations and the ghetto disturbances which took place in the summer of 1966, Daley appointed a twenty-three member citizens committee to hold public hearings on ways of improving relations between the Police Department and the public. Significantly, the committee could find little basis for criticizing the police. It found, for example, that "During the trying occasions in Chicago in the summer of 1966 (on the basis of the Chairman's 'on the scene' observations) the Chicago police conducted themselves with commendable restraint, courage, common sense and competence. . . . In short, they were objective professionals." [1]

The same tone was set in other internal reviews which broached the role of the police in the city's slums. In response to allegations of police brutality, a 1966 study sponsored by the Chicago Bar Association and Police Superintendent Orlando Wilson found that during the period covering November 1, 1956 to June 30, 1966, the overwhelming number of complaints against the police—433 out of 469 to be exact—were either unfounded or could not be sustained.[2] And after the damaging ghetto riots of April, 1968, Mayor Daley appointed still another investigative committee which absolved the police of any wrongdoing though it did recommend new mass arrest procedures.[3]

This is in contrast to federal and state reports which were warning of police abuses in the ghetto. During the 1966–69 period, two such efforts on the federal level were hearings conducted by the Illinois Advisory Committee of the U.S. Commission on Civil Rights and a U.S. Justice Department financed study by Yale Professor Albert J. Reiss.[4] The Illinois Division of the American Civil Liberties Union report of the police during a peace march in the Spring of 1968 summed-up the tenor of these critiques: "Brutalizing demonstrators without provocation, they (the police) failed to live up to that difficult professionalism which we demand." [5]

Even more indicative of the politics of civil review in Chicago is the chain of inquiries which came about after the Democratic National Convention disorders of August, 1968. Witnessed by a national television audience, a series of clashes between police and demonstrators provoked heated commentary and criticism throughout the country. Anticipating federal government investigations into charges of police beatings, Mayor Daley ordered his own inquiry to be directed by Raymond F. Simon, the City's Corporation Counsel. Cooperating with Simon were the Chicago police, the City Law Department and the United States Attorney's office.

Entitled "The Strategy of Confrontation," the final report was issued on September 6, less than a week after the Convention ended, and described itself "not as a defense of the city of Chicago but primarily as an effort to point out the nature and strategy of confrontation as it was employed in Chicago."[6] Among the many facts presented were lists of weapons used by the protestors, a breakdown of the number and nature of injuries of civilians and policemen (according to the report, 60 civilians and 161 policemen were injured), and an accounting of the clashes between the police and demonstrators in Grant and Lincoln parks and in front of the Conrad Hilton hotel, the headquarters of the convention. Referring to the leaders of the disturbances, the report warned that "their ultimate goal, also publicly proclaimed, was to topple what they consider to be the corrupt institutions of our society, educational, governmental, etc., by impeding and if possible halting their normal functions while exposing the authorities to ridicule and embarrassment."[7] The report concluded by criticizing the media for attributing "malice to the authorities while presuming good will and sincerity on the part of the protestors."[8]

Approximately two days prior to the publication of the Chicago document, it was announced in Washington that President Lyndon B. Johnson's new Commission on the Causes and Prevention of Violence would also investigate the disorders. The Commission's chairman, Dr. Milton Eisenhower, explained that the decision for such an undertaking was made without consulting President Johnson and that it would not be a political investigation even though the disorders occurred during the Democratic National Convention. Shortly thereafter he contracted with Daniel Walker, a prominent Chicago attorney and president of the prestigious Chicago Crime Commission, to conduct the inquiry. The final report called "Rights in Conflict" was released on December 2, 1968 after fifty-three days of furious effort. Taking notice, in the foreward, of the conflicting responses to the Chicago disturbances ("The Strategy of Confrontation" was given as one example), the task force explained its reason for being: "Our purpose is to present the facts so that thoughtful readers can decide what lessons come out of them; for it is urgent that any such lessons be speedily incorporated into American public life."[9]

But the facts presented an interpretation quite different from the one offered by the Daley administration. While admitting that "the Chicago Police were the targets of mounting provocation by both word and act," the Walker report asserted that "The nature of the response was unrestrained and indiscriminate police violence on many occasions, particularly at night. That violence was made all the more shocking by the fact that it was often inflicted upon persons who had broken no law, disobeyed no order, made no threat."[10] Nor could the city administration be absolved of complicity. For example, the report credits the police with restraint in handling earlier rioting which followed the death of Dr. Martin Luther King and the April 27th peace march to the Civic Center in Chicago. ". . . but Mayor Daley rebuked the Superintendent of Police. While it was later modified, his widely disseminated 'shoot to kill arsonists and shoot to maim looters' order undoubtedly had an effect. The effect on police became apparent several weeks later when they attacked demonstrators, bystanders and media representatives at a Civic Center peace march."[11] The Walker team also noted that since the Democratic convention disorders, "There has been no public condemnation of these violators of sound police procedures and common decency by either their commanding officers or city officials."[12]

In the meanwhile, a third major inquiry was initiated on September 9 when Chief Judge William J. Campbell of the Federal District Court in Chicago ordered a federal grand jury to investigate the convention disturbances. After seven months of hearings, sixteen persons were indicted: eight leaders of the demonstrations were charged with conspiracy to incite a riot and eight policemen were charged with assault and perjury. In answer to a question about the equal number of indictments of policeman and demonstrators, United States Attorney Thomas A. Foran denied there was any truth to published reports that the Justice Department wanted to "balance indictments of demonstrators and policemen so that the grand jury would not seem to be blaming the police for the violence that racked Chicago during the week of August 25."[13] Although the validity of Attorney Foran's reply cannot be verified, it is instructive that it was the federal jurisdiction and not Chicago government that succeeded in charging eight Chicago policemen.[a]

The pattern of review in which outside sources indict while inside sources protect has persisted even under the most controversial of circumstances. Thus, another issue that has not yet been fully resolved pertains to a predawn police raid of December 4, 1969 on a Black Panther apartment. On that occasion, a detachment of Chicago police assigned to the State's Attorney's office, shot and killed Black Panther leader Fred Hampton and Panther lieutenant Mark Clark. Seven other Panthers were arrested. The police found contraband weapons and ammunition that they were looking for and, though there were the usual cries of "police brutality," the incident seemed closed. But as time passed, questions multiplied and more and more people became dissatisfied with the

[a]None of the policemen were ever convicted. However, while five of the demonstrators were convicted of crossing state lines to incite rioting, they were eventually acquitted in a federal court. Subsequently three of the demonstrators were found guilty of Contempt of Court.

answers. To find out what "really" happened, a series of inquiries were begun leading to different but nevertheless revealing results.

First, a special county coroner's jury was sworn in and, after twelve days investigation, returned a finding of justifiable homicide in the deaths of Hampton and Clark. The police and the State's Attorney Edward V. Hanrahan appeared vindicated. But events took a dramatic turn when the Justice Department's federal grand jury released its report on May 15, 1970. It found that the raiding party had fired eighty-two to ninety-nine shots into the apartment and received at most one shot in return. This was in direct contradiction to Hanrahan's reenactment of the "shoot-out" for the news reporters and for television. Criticism was also directed toward the Chicago Police Department over the way in which it later investigated the matter. The jury, however, returned no indictments though some of its findings, particularly the one about the number of shots fired, raised still more questions.

Community pressure for another inquiry continued to build and on June 20, 1970, the presiding judge of the County Criminal Court, Joseph A. Power, a former law partner and neighbor of Mayor Daley, appointed a special county grand jury and a special prosecutor to handle a new investigation.[b] The prosecutor was Barnabas F. Sears, a distinguished Chicago Lawyer who had performed a similar role in the 1960 scandal involving police collusion with burglars. The twenty-three jurors met regularly and heard witnesses from December of 1970 into the Spring of 1971. In late April, the story leaked out that the jurors had voted true bills (i.e., endorsements saying the evidence warrants a criminal charge) against a number of persons, including Hanrahan, and that it had attempted to return them as an indictment before Power on April 22. But Power refused to accept the indictment, and ordered the jury to hear testimony from Hanrahan and also from a number of other witnesses who had appeared before the federal grand jury but not before the county grand jury. Hanrahan had declined an invitation to appear earlier before the county jury.

On April 26, in Power's courtroom, Sears agreed to bring Hanrahan before the jury, but refused to subpoena the other witnesses on the grounds that they had nothing to add to testimony already heard. This did not satisfy Judge Power, however, who decided to fine Sears fifty dollars an hour around the clock for refusing to call the witnesses, and one hundred dollars for "contemptuous" remarks Sears allegedly had made to the press on April 22. At the same time, attorneys for those reportedly named by the grand jury filed a petition asking that the grand jury be dismissed because it had been "tainted" by published

---

[b]This investigation is not included in our data in Table 3-1 since it did not occur during the 1966-1969 period.

accounts of the controversy. They also charged that Sears had improperly "pressured" the jurors to indict.

Months of intricate legal maneuvering followed. On June 23 Sears appealed to the Illinois Supreme Court and succeeded in nullifying both contempt citations against him. In August, Sears went back to the Supreme Court to win an order compelling Judge Power to accept and make public the grand jury's action. As finally promulgated on August 24, 1971, the indictment accused Mr. Hanrahan and thirteen others—eight raiding policemen, Hanrahan's assistant in charge of the special police force, and police officials in charge of departmental investigations—of knowingly conspiring to obstruct justice by attempting to thwart criminal prosecution of the eight policemen who participated in the raid. The indictment also specifically accused Hanrahan of presenting evidence before another Cook County grand jury that "he knew or reasonably should have known to be false and inflammatory." [14] He had done this, the grand jury charged, to get the indictment of the seven survivors. (All charges against the seven had been dropped by Hanrahan after the federal grand jury's presentment.) In addition, Chicago's Police Superintendent James B. Conlisk Jr., two other assistant state's attorneys, and two police officers involved in a postraid investigation, were named as coconspirators but not as defendants.

Nor, as yet, have conflicting accounts ceased to come forth. Another report by a special blue–ribbon commission of nationally prominent persons was leaked to the press in March of 1972.[c] (Former Attorney General Ramsey Clark and NAACP Executive Director Roy Wilkens were cochairman of this group called the Commission of Inquiry into the Black Panthers and Law Enforcement.) It contended that "neither the federal government nor the state sought to establish the truth." [15] It found that Illinois Black Panther Chairman Fred Hampton "was shot from the doorway to his bedroom as he lay drugged and defenseless in bed." Dr. David M. Spain, a New York pathologist, who participated in an autopsy on Hampton's body, is quoted as saying: "The integrity of the Cook County coroner's office is open to serious question. . . . The pathologist who performed the autopsy testified that he had opened the stomach of the corpse and examined its contents. . . . At the third autopsy, it was found that the stomach was completely closed and had never been opened." [16] Furthermore, while the Commission of Inquiry's report agreed with the federal grand jury that the Panthers had fired only one shot during the raid, it makes this additional finding: "The one shot fired out (by the Panthers) was not the first shot. The first shot was fired by the police." [17]

Almost as an anti-climax, Hanrahan and his thirteen codefendants were acquitted by Chicago Circuit Court Judge Philip J. Romiti on October 26,

[c]We do not include this in our data in Table 3–1. At the time of writing, neither the report nor the investigation had been completed.

1972. After listening to the prosecution for thirteen weeks, the Judge's ruling was simple: No defense witnesses were needed because "evidence is simply not sufficient to establish or prove any conspiracy against any of the defendants."[18]

New York City

While Chicago has been protective of its police force, New York City appears to lean in a very different direction. Table 3-1 shows that ten out of twelve civil reviews which occurred between 1966 and 1969 were authorized by forces internal to the city and seven of these were essentially critical. (See Appendix A for a listing of reviews.)

In 1966 and 1967, internal reviews appeared as essentially professional critiques. Yet, covered in these analyses were some very sensitive issues which would eventually foment acrimony with the police establishment. Typifying this were the efforts of the Law Enforcement Task Force, an eight-man study group appointed by Mayor John V. Lindsay during the first year of his administration. Analyzing police procedures, the Task Force denounced nepotism in the appointment of detectives and "petty, unnecessary, hyper-detailed and unrealistic" regulations. It accused the police department of "many practices that are either outmoded, inefficient or undesirable."[19] On questions of law enforcement in the city, the panel advocated the appointment of a special assistant to the Mayor who would coordinate the work of all law enforcement agencies. It also urged the consolidation of the five District Attorneys' officers in the city and revision of the courts and probation procedures. But what proved to be the bombshell, as measured by police reaction, was the recommendation that a civilian–controlled board should review police actions in response to civilian complaints. As we shall see in the next section, this proposal quickly escalated into one of the most bitterly argued of city issues.

Shortly after the appointment of Howard R. Leary as the new Police Commissioner in February, 1966, two other inquiries were initiated. Leary asked the Vera Foundation, a private research group which had been studying court procedures, to study police methods of handling suspects from the moment of arrest until their arraignment in court. At about the same time, Lindsay commissioned the International Association of Chiefs of Police to study the operations and management of the police Department.

There was little that the police or anyone else could say against the final recommendations of the Vera Foundation effort—a plan which would reduce the holding of suspects in precinct cells by releasing those arrested for minor offenses with a summons to appear in court at a later date. Indeed,

Commissioner Leary soon put the proposal into effect. But the I.A.C.P. report, calling for a top-to-bottom reorganization of New York's Police Department, provoked considerable controversy. The basic recommendation was that the present scattered functional agencies of the Department be reorganized into five bureaus—personnel, administration, field operations, technical services and inspections. Somewhat more controversial was the suggestion that the position of Chief Inspector, the department's top uniformed officer, be abolished and that the Commissioner should function as a chief of police. This was unacceptable to Mayor Lindsay who, with Leary, had appointed Sanford D. Garelick to that office over the opposition of other ranking police officers. The I.A.C.P. report also stated that a misreading of the slogan "New York's finest" had led people to assume that the police were the finest in the country—an assumption "that has been allowed to inhibit organizational and procedural improvements within the department." [20] It was this last statement, particularly, that drew the ire of the Patrolmen's Benevolent Association. Over the long run, there was little in this report which was ever actually put into practice.

In 1968 and 1969 public inquiries into police affairs became much more controversial in nature. During this time, three different county grand jury investigations were conducted into such sensitive matters as police corruption and police abuse of citizens. The New York American Civil Liberties Union released a study which accused the police of arbitrary methods of arrest. An inquiry by the City Controller and the City Corporation Counsel into the Patrolmen's Benevolent Association's health and welfare fund led to allegations of irregularities. As a result of such efforts, a number of policemen were subsequently convicted and two ranking P.B.A. officials resigned from office. We should note, further, that only the RAND Corporation's systems analysis of police communications appears to have been devoid of any accusations or recriminations.

In contrast to Chicago, police reviews originating outside New York City were minimal. During the entire period 1966 to 1969, there were only two separate hearings by state legislative committees: one inquired into the role and legal status of the John Birch Society in the New York City Police Department; the other considered the general problem of how the police are expected to perform in riots. In the former case, a recommendation was made by the committee that all John Birch members be expelled from the police.[d]

To a significant extent, the pattern of review we've described sets the tone for much of what follows in New York. Criticism of the police origi-

[d]This issue is treated below in Chapter 5.

nates with the Mayor, the Commissioner he appointed, and allied parties. Contrary to the other two cities being studied, the organized police bureaucracy of New York has had to learn to protect itself without the assistance of City Hall.

Philadelphia

Civil review in Philadelphia shows some important differences with what we discerned for either Chicago or New York. Most obvious in Table 3-1, is the fact that civil oversight of the police has been exercised less frequently in Philadelphia than in the other two cities. Just as important is the finding that critical reviews have also occurred less frequently. (See Appendix B for a listing of reviews.)

Closer inspection shows that the only three negative critiques which originated outside of the city took place early in 1966. Two of these—a federal grand jury probe of racketeering and a Pennsylvania state legislative committee investigating narcotics—claimed to show some degree of police collusion with gamblers and narcotic pushers. The third critique was a staff study prepared for the President's Commission on Law Enforcement and Administration of Justice which cited a "lackadaisical" attitude and some dishonesty among Philadelphia's police.[21]

In each case, the report, or follow-up attempts to effect change in light of the report, was criticized or refuted by the Police Commissioner, the Mayor and others who ranked high in the police establishment. The pattern of refutation was generally the same. The Police Department would assume the responsibility of investigating allegations made by the outside agencies and would subsequently report no validating revelations. Strong supporting pronouncements served to preclude further inquiry from any other source.

After 1966, five reviews originated from within the city with some interesting results. Where inquiries were initiated by the Mayor or other city officials, findings tended to be supportive of the police role. For example, in November of 1967, Mayor Tate authorized an inquiry into charges of police brutality stemming from school demonstrations in which a number of black students had been hurt.[e] Tate appointed himself, Fred T. Corleto, the city's Managing Director, and City Solicitor Edward G. Bauer, Jr. to the investigating committee and after several days reported that the police and the Board of Education had settled their differences over various allegations. The question of whether or not police brutality had actually occurred as a finding of fact was simply ignored. In 1968 and again in 1969, the Police Department contracted with the Franklin Institute, a private research organization, to undertake two

[e]This is discussed in greater detail in Chapter 4.

different studies of its organizational status. In each case, the Department passed muster with high professional ratings and recommendations for increased manpower.

Of some significance is the fact that in the entire four-year period, only two internal reviews ever offered any criticism of the city's police force. A "State of the City Report" by the Philadelphia Chapter of Americans for Democratic Action expressed concern over the deterioration of police-community relations in the city, and the "arrogance, lack of neutrality, and violence" exhibited in tense situations such as in school demonstrations.[22] The other critical review was an unreleased report by the city's Commission on Human Relations which catalogued police abuses in the ghetto community. The Commission's executive director, Clarence Farmer, had attempted to keep the report quiet, but it was nevertheless leaked by the staff. In attempting to justify his behavior, Mr. Farmer explained that "there were some things in it that would really upset some people like the Police Commissioner."[23]

Viewed overall, Philadelphia appears to compare more closely with Chicago where the source of police criticism has been external, than with New York City where critical reports have been sponsored by forces well-rooted in the city's politics. Like Chicago, the city of Philadelphia and its administration appeared to be protective of its police. Unlike Chicago, however, critical assessments from outside sources seemed to have disappeared after 1966.

WHO RULES THE POLICE?

Table 3-2 provides us with a broader perspective into the subject of civil review and accountability. In the previous section, we were essentially interested in determining the extent to which the civil authorities exercised watchfulness over the police activities of our sample communities. In this section, we are interested in discerning influence patterns: we identify actors who successfully initiate review proposals or veto review proposals by others. Such an approach permits us to locate those persons or groups to whom the police are actually accountable, irrespective of the formal lines of command.

Our data consists of cases already identified in Table 3-1, such as who initiates or vetoes reviews, as well as other cases which deal with decisions on review procedures, such as questions on methods of overseeing the police. For example, an issue which has provoked a great deal of controversy in New York City and Philadelphia is the argument over the alleged advantages and disadvantages of civilian review boards. Complaining of police brutality, blacks and civil rights groups have become dissatisfied with procedures of internal police review. They have proposed, instead, the use of civilian dominated boards to investigate and judge citizen complaints against police behavior. The police,

Table 3-2. Civil Review and Accountability of Police: Leaders

	New York City		Philadelphia		Chicago	
	Successes	*Defeats*	*Successes*	*Defeats*	*Successes*	*Defeats*
Mayor	7	4	4	—	5	—
Cmmr./Supt.	7	5	2	—	2	3**
Police officers/Dept.	0	3**	2	1**	—	—
Policemen's assns.	4	6	3	1	—	***
Others	<u>10</u>	***	<u>6</u>	***	<u>12</u>	***
Total successes*	28	***	17	***	19	***

*Number of successes do not equal the total number of decisions as more than one person can be attributed with having been successful in a particular decision.

**This includes damaging revelations *via* civil review of police malpractices, e.g., corruption.

***Not estimated.

in turn, have vehemently resisted with the counter-argument that only police-men have the professional capabilities of judging policemen.

Another important issue here pertains to the question: to whom should the police be accountable? As we discussed the matter in a previous chapter, reformers have developed a rationale of professional independence to defend the police jurisdiction from the politicians. The fact that the police department is expected to be "politically independent," however, raises some serious questions about the extent to which mayors and other high officials are to be responsible for police actions.

New York City
During the heyday of Tammany Hall, the New York City Police Department was heavily implicated in political favoritism and promotions as illustrated by the comment of Mayor John P. O'Brien, in 1933. When asked who the new Police Commissioner was going to be, Mr. O'Brien reportedly said: "I don't know, I haven't got the word yet."

Political interference continued during the reform administration of Mayor Fiorello H. LaGuardia, only this time it came directly from the Mayor himself. According to the testimony of former commissioner Francis W.H. Adams, the Department "suffered most" under Mayor LaGuardia, who "inter-fered with everything, from the appointment of deputy commissioners on down." It wasn't until Mayor Robert Wagner took office in 1954 that the De-partment was made truly autonomous. "Mr. Wagner never made any suggestion to me at any time in any respect," Mr. Adams said.[24]

By the 1960's, however, as the police came under attack by Negro and Puerto Rican groups, Wagner's hands-off policy became much less tenable. It fell to Mayor John Lindsay, who was elected in 1965, to define a new rela-tionship between City Hall and the police. The data in Table 3-2 gives some measure of Lindsay's strivings to assert his command authority. If Lindsay appears to have had difficulty, comparing successes with defeats, it is to be noted that so, too, did the police commissioners who served under him.

Perhaps no issue reflects the complexities of this subject as does the civilian review board controversy. In the mayoralty campaign of 1965, Lindsay promised that, if elected, he would appoint a board of civilians and police to judge allegations of police brutality. But whether this was "supervision," as Lindsay preferred to call it, or "interference" as the Police Commissioner alleged, was a question that provoked vehement debate.

As noted earlier, the proposal to create a civilian review board in New York City was made by Lindsay's Law Enforcement Task Force in its report of February 6, 1966. Taking its cues from the Mayor's election campaign, the Task Force recommended that a controlling majority of four outside civilians be added to the existing Police Department Civilian Complaint Review Board staffed by three deputy commissioners. Opposition crystallized almost immediately from the person of Police Commissioner Vincent Broderick, a holdover from the Wagner administration, as well as from the Patrolmen's Benevolent Association. While Lindsay was able to cope with the Commissioner as a source of resistance, he had much greater difficulty in dealing with the P.B.A.

When Mayor Lindsay announced the appointment of a new Commissioner on February 15, it was of surprise to no one including Broderick whose term was expiring. The new appointee was Howard R. Leary who, as Police Commissioner of Philadelphia, had garnered praise from civil rights leaders for his cooperation with that city's civilian review board. Though Lindsay could justify his action under the City Charter, Broderick and former commissioner Francis W.H. Adams alleged that, indirectly, it constituted political interference in the Police Department. Leary, they contended, would be a stranger in the city and would not know whom to appoint as deputy commissioners and inspectors. "He will have to refer to his friends at City Hall, who are the only people he knows. It seems to me that this is opening the door to political interference in the Police Department." [25]

On the day that Howard Leary was sworn in, Lindsay took extra care to defend his role in police affairs. In his address, he insisted that "the Mayor's responsibilities in law enforcement matters are clear cut" and stated: [26]

> These desperate voices which have spoken in the past weeks about the relationship between the Police Department and the Mayor have come perilously close to missing the basic principle of a democratically elected government.
>
> They have suggested—no, they have stated—that the Police Department is a law unto itself. They have stated that the duly elected civilian government of New York is not responsible for the Police Department as it is for the other departments of the city. . . .
>
> The ultimate responsibility lies with the Mayor, and I intend to exercise that responsibility.

Lindsay's real problems were yet to come. In a television interview on February 20, P.B.A. President John J. Cassese said that his group was prepared to spend its whole treasury of $1.5 million to fight a civilian–controlled review board. The signal to begin this effort came on May 2 when the Mayor and Commissioner Leary jointly announced the creation of a Civilian Complaint Review Board by executive order. The plan called for the Board to have three police officials and four civilians with a civilian executive director, plus its own investigating unit of police officers and conciliation procedures. The civilians would be appointed by the Mayor. The Board, however, would not be able to recommend specific punishments for policemen but would recommend whether the Police Department should prefer charges. Should the Department accept the recommendation, the officer would get a departmental hearing prosecuted and judged solely by the police.

The P.B.A. leadership countered quickly by introducing a bill in the New York State Legislature aimed at blocking civilian review. When that failed, they petitioned the New York State Supreme Court charging that the plan was "illegal and invalid" and would create a "kangaroo court." When the Court upheld the plan as within the legal authority of the Police Commissioner, the P.B.A. pushed ahead with a campaign to put the whole question of a civilian review board before the city's voters in a referendum vote at the next general election. It was anticipated that through this mechanism, the City Charter would be amended to limit board membership to the Police Department.

On July 7, 1966 the P.B.A. filed 51,852 signatures with the City Clerk; and in a separate action the New York Conservative Party filed 40,383 signatures for a similar amendment to be placed on the ballot. The City Clerk, however, ruled both petitions invalid on the grounds that restrictions on the Commissioner's powers are a matter for the Administrative Code which do not require approval by the voters. The decision was short-lived. A series of legal appeals culminating in New York's highest Court, the Court of Appeals, overruled the City Clerk and permitted the P.B.A. proposal to remain on the ballot. To avoid confusion, the Conservative Party then withdrew its petition.

This cleared the way, then, for a direct electoral battle between the administration and the P.B.A. The opponents of civilian review were organized into the Independent Citizens Committee Against Review Boards, with the P.B.A. as the dominant organization. Administration supporters were organized into the Federated Associations for Impartial Review (FAIR) and was dominated by the New York American Civil Liberties Union. The principle argument of the former was that the Board would impair the morale and efficiency of the police force and, as a consequence, increase crime in the streets. FAIR denied such claims and argued that in Philadelphia, the crime rate had declined after a similar board had been instituted. FAIR also contended that civilians on the Board would restore public confidence in the police.

On November 8, 1966, the electorate decided the issue. The Civilian Complaint Review Board was overwhelming rejected by a vote of 1,313,161 (63 percent) to 765,468 (36 percent). Neighborhood districts with heavy concentrations of black and Hispanic persons clearly favored the retention of the Review Board. But these areas with a few others were isolated districts when compared to prevailing sentiments in the rest of the city.

In the aftermath of their defeat, the Lindsay administration attempted to salvage something from the original Review Board proposal. On November 22, 1966, Commissioner Leary announced a new intradepartmental body which would take over the name, address, staff and responsibilities of the Civilian Complaint Review Board. At the same time he appointed five senior officials to the Board: Three of the men were civilian employees of the Police Department; two others were deputy commissioners who, in police terms, were also civilians since they were not members of the uniformed police or detectives.

Such action did not endear Lindsay to the police, for it was he who was generally acknowledged as Leary's guiding spirit. In retaliation, the P.B.A. and allied police organizations continued to use the allegation of "political interference" against the Mayor. The opportunity to capitalize on this strategy came along soon enough during antidraft demonstrations in December of 1967. Anticipating violence, the Mayor had instructed two of his assistants, Barry Gottehrer and Sid Davidoff, to walk with the demonstrators and to act as liaison between them and the police.

The P.B.A. leadership took a different view of this, however, and in a telecast interview, President Cassese asserted that the two mayoralty assistants should resign because they "were trying to intimidate the policemen." He said that "they put themselves at the head of the line" and that "they said, 'We're from the Mayor's office.' "[27] Norman Frank, the P.B.A. community–relations counsel, contended that as a result of their behavior, the police "certainly could not act in the manner that they thought would be most constructive in controlling this demonstration."[28] Mr. Frank continued:

> I think City Hall is actively calling policy. . . . and has involved itself in all areas of Police Department activity, and I want to underscore this in the face of professional objections in the Police Department, because the people who are interfering at the highest levels have no background in law enforcement.[29]

For the second time in twenty–one months, Lindsay was compelled to defend his police role. In rebuffing the P.B.A., the Mayor advanced the theory that he is the chief executive of the city and therefore his relationship with the Police Commissioner should be the same as the President's relationship with ranking military advisers. "I believe the Mayor has a role to play in the fixing of policy in all matters in the city. We have a policy role to fill, just as the President does with the Joint Chiefs of Staff."[30]

In spite of this pronouncement, the dispute over who sets police policy continued and reached a new crescendo in the Summer of 1968, a period of unsettlement following the assassination of the Reverend Martin Luther King, Jr. Repeating his old charge that Lindsay had been restraining the police, P.B.A. President John Cassese directed his membership to disregard orders from superior officers to refrain from arresting looters, vandals, unruly demonstrators and other law violators. At the same time, he promised to issue new "get tough" guidelines to his men calling for arrests "regardless of what orders we may get from any superior officer." [31]

On the day that Cassese was to announce his rules, Commissioner Leary issued a teletype order to all commands, warning of prompt disciplinary action to all who do not respond to orders. This time, it was the Police Commissioner who was defining his role:

> According to law—the City Charter and the City Administrative Code—the Police Commissioner is given the power and the authority and the duty to run the Police Department. This includes the making of policy, the practices and the administration of the department. While this authority can be delegated to a subordinate member of the Police Department, the responsibility always remains with the Police Commissioner, who has the obligation to see that this delegated authority is properly executed.[32]

When Cassese finally issued the anticipated P.B.A. guidelines, it was apparent that he had backed away. They were nothing more than excerpts from the penal law and Police Department regulations. But if Cassese had retreated, it was also clear that he retreated from a position unprecedented in the history of the New York police force. Never before had the police bureaucracy asserted itself to that extent.

Philadelphia

New York is not the only city which has debated the issue of political control of the Police Department. Prior to the Clark-Dilworth reform era which began in 1952, observers of Philadelphia politics agree that "no major policy decision or personnel promotion was made in the Police Department without the approval of the Mayor and the 'politicians' out in the wards. This surely included . . . promotion and assignment of District Police Captains." [33] Cleaning the politics out of the Police Department has been rated one of the most notable of the Clark-Dilworth achievements.

When James H.J. Tate moved from the City Council into City Hall to succeed Richardson Dilworth, it soon became evident that the old reform nostrum of "no political interference" would become problematic once again. In contrast to either Clark or Dilworth, Tate himself was a product of the Democratic machine. Furthermore, like other big cities, Philadelphia and its police force were beginning to feel new pressures from its rapidly growing black population and, in fact, soon experienced a major riot in its black districts in 1964.

It was the way Mayor Tate appointed a new police commissioner in the Spring of 1966 that caused some stir among the "good government" elements of the city. When Mayor Lindsay of New York City chose Philadelphia's Commissioner Howard Leary to be the head of New York's Police Department, Deputy Commissioner Edward J. Bell was appointed Acting Commissioner of the Philadelphia force. Tate then set up a special committee of distinguished citizens to screen and recommend candidates for the available post. During the time that the committee was deliberating, however, the Mayor publicized his preference for Bell and also indicated that the committee shared this preference. The committee, however, felt that it was being misrepresented; and instead of recommending Bell, who had received the public endorsement of the press, the Fraternal Order of Police, and various ethnic group organizations, it submitted the name of the chief of police of a medium–size western city. Bell's name was submitted along with four others as being "also qualified." Consequently, Tate was made to overrule his own committee. As one observer comments, "this conflict was unfortunate for Commissioner Bell, for it tended to diminish the 'nonpolitical' aura of his appointment. It could have tended to diminish the independence of action which the new commissioner would need upon assuming his post." [34]

The civilian review board controversy soon posed a more fundamental challenge to the leadership of both Tate and the Commissioner; and this time the principle source of challenge was Philadelphia's Fraternal Order of Police, Lodge 5. This is demonstrated in Table 3–2 where we see the F.O.P. scoring almost as many successes in matters of civil review and accountability as the Mayor and one more than the Commissioner. All of the F.O.P.'s victories here are the result of a series of battles over Philadelphia's Police Advisory Board (P.A.B.).

The first of its kind in the country, the Board was created on October 1, 1958 by executive order of Mayor Richardson Dilworth and given the responsibility of:

> . . . considering citizens' complaints against the police where the charges involve brutality, false arrest, discrimination based upon religion or national origin or other wrongful conduct of police personnel toward citizens. [35]

The creation of the Board came after a long period of citizen dissatisfaction with existing channels for redress of grievances against policemen. The black population of Philadelphia was especially vehement in complaining about the ineffectuality of pressing complaints through the Police Department. Because the City Council refused to establish the Board by ordinance, it came into existence by order of the Mayor in an atmosphere of controversy; and persistent attacks by the Fraternal Order of Police and its President, John J. Harrington, served to keep the controversy alive. In resisting civilian review of police work, the policemen's association maintained that the Police Advisory Board harasses the police, lowers their morale and reduces their effectiveness. Harrington even posed the theory that Philadelphia's 1964 riot could be attributed to the fact that, at the time, the city was the only one in the nation with a civilian–staffed review board. That the P.A.B. was merely an advisory board to the Mayor which could only make recommendations after a public hearing did not impress the F.O.P. at all.

In 1959, the F.O.P. filed a suit challenging the Board's legality, but withdrew it after the Board agreed to a list of procedural changes. But six years later, in September 1965, the F.O.P. filed another suit asking abolition of the Board. Winning a temporary injunction which halted the work of the P.A.B. for five months, the F.O.P. tried again with another judge and this time it succeeded. On March 29, 1967, Judge Leo Weinrott of Common Pleas Court found that the Board took upon itself the functions of a judicial tribunal rather than that of an advisory board and that it rendered judgments which in practical effect were equivalent to judicial orders. He also agreed with the F.O.P. contention that the P.A.B. had no right to expunge a complainant's arrest record. This was done in cases where the complainant had been arrested and charges were later dropped. On the basis of the evidence, the Judge stated that "The very existence of the board, the harassment of officers and the anxiety which its existence promotes must inevitably lessen the effectiveness of police performance."[36] Primarily for these reasons, then, and because the City Charter gives disciplinary responsibility only to the Police Department, Judge Weinrott ruled the P.A.B. illegal and void.

After nineteen months delay, the City Law Department filed exceptions to Judge Weinrott's decision as the first stage of appeal. Generally, exceptions are heard by a panel of three judges including the one who made the original ruling. But in this case Weinrott heard them again by himself, because, he said, neither side had requested a panel of three judges. As could have been expected, Weinrott dismissed the exceptions in an opinion similar to the earlier one. The city then appealed to the Pennsylvania Supreme Court and, surprisingly, in June of 1969, the Supreme Court overruled Judge Weinrott by a five to two decision. Speaking for the majority, Justice Herbert B. Cohen stressed the fact that the P.A.B.'s powers were strictly advisory and the Judge Weinrott strayed from the legal issues in handing down his finding. The Police Advisory Board, therefore, was legal.

But all was not lost for the F.O.P. If the policemen's organization appeared to have been defeated in the courts, Mayor Tate came to its rescue. Right after the judicial decision which justified reactivation of the P.A.B., Tate took a vacation in Europe and sent back word that he saw no reason for haste in deciding the future of the agency. When he returned from his vacation in July, Tate was prepared to clarify what many had begun to suspect: "It's about time we began to support our Police Department. So far as I'm concerned it (the Board) is on the shelf. I see no reason to reactivate it at this time." Some five months later, when P.A.B. members attempted to revive the Board with the assistance of a volunteer staff, Tate was prepared to take the final step. Visiting police headquarters to wish officers and their families a Merry Christmas, he read a one line executive order he had signed. It said: "The Philadelphia Police Advisory Board created October 1, 1958, by letters of appointment, is hereby dissolved."[38] The announcement brought a one–minute standing ovation from the police officials in the audience.

In assessing the roles of the Mayor and the Police Commissioner, that which is most striking is the shift from an attitude of tolerance towards the idea of civilian review to one of opposition. During his first term in office (1963 to 1967), Tate openly expressed the view that the board protected the police from abuse as well as the public. Tate's commissioners, Howard Leary and Edward Bell, also evidenced willingness to cooperate. But a new perspective becomes noticeable after Tate's reelection in November, 1967. At that time, he was reluctant to press for an appeal of Judge Weinrott's Common Pleas Court decision which upheld the F.O.P. suit against the Police Advisory Board. Interviews reveal that the only reason Tate agreed to appeal to the State Supreme Court was his assumption, after consultation, that Weinrott's decision would be upheld. When this strategy failed, Tate was forced to come out into the open and make a decision he was hoping to avoid.

Speculation on the circumstances which induced this change of attitude towards the P.A.B. would have to refer to Tate's uphill political battle and his narrow margin of victory in the election of 1967. For it is unlikely that he could have won without devising a new "get–tough" strategy during a time of racial unrest. Having been denied his party's endorsement, Tate appointed Frank L. Rizzo to replace the ailing Edward Bell to the position of Police Commissioner. Widely known as a "no–nonsense" policeman and someone notorious to civil rights groups, Rizzo became an important political symbol. Using Rizzo's reputation in his campaign, Tate unexpectedly won both the primary and the regular election. The F.O.P. leadership claimed part of the credit: "Tate won by only 12,000 votes and we think its because we went out on a limb. Police and firemen, wives and families—that's 50,000 votes."[39]

Thereafter, the Tate–Rizzo–F.O.P. coalition functioned with surprising cohesiveness. Having achieved success in this important area, the coalition, as we shall see, continued to operate on other fronts. Contrary to the New York City experience, moreover, Mayor Tate of Philadelphia felt no need to promulgate a chief-executive theory of police supervision. Rather, after the coming of Rizzo, the theme of "police independence" was resurrected as among the important principles for administering the city.

Chicago

Table 3-2 shows that the pattern of command and control of the police in Chicago contrasts significantly with what has been discerned for either New York City or Philadelphia. Mayor Daley rules with no competition from others in the city, nor is there any evidence of opposition from the city's policemen's organizations. The only real challenge to the Mayor's authority comes from sources outside of the city such as a federally sponsored inquiry or a federal grand jury investigation. (This comprises the bulk of the "others" category in Table 3-2.)

The protective posture of City Hall towards the police is of special significance in accounting for the strong leadership role of Chicago's Mayor. As we noted in the previous section, reviews of police behavior which originate from outside the city are essentially critical while most reviews which are internal to the city are supportive of the police. This has been achieved through the careful maneuvering of Mayor Daley himself. Whenever criticism of the police has been anticipated, the Mayor has used his authority to appoint a competing investigatory group for countervailing effect. Thus "The Strategy of Confrontation" anticipated probable challenges to the police in "Rights in Conflict."

A related factor in accounting for the Mayor's strong command role is the fact that the issue of civil review of the police, which has caused so much controversy in Philadelphia and New York, has never been seriously considered in the governing institutions of Chicago. In spite of demands by black and libertarian groups for an independent reviewing agency, the processing of complaints against the police is a function which the police control. The Mayor also participates indirectly. If a citizen believes that a policeman has used excessive force against him, he can file a complaint with the Department's Internal Affairs Division (IAD). More serious cases are considered by the Chicago Police Board which consists of five civilians appointed by the Mayor with the approval of the City Council. As a sop to some of his critics, Daley established another office in January of 1969 called the Registrar of Citizens' Complaints—a civilian appointed by the Mayor. A citizen who is not satisfied with action taken by the other units can request a further review by the Registrar.

Critics have described the IAD as "the world's biggest washing machine." That opinion was reinforced by the report in May, 1970 by the federal grand jury that investigated the deaths of two Black Panther leaders during the police raid of December 4, 1969. The grand jury stated that it had insufficient evidence to accuse the police raiders of willful violation of civil rights. But it did charge that an IAD investigation of the raid "Was so seriously deficient that it suggests purposeful malfeasance." The federal report found that the police from the IAD assigned to investigate the case had met with the raiders and members of the State's Attorney's office and had drawn up an authorized set of questions and answers. Superintendent Conlisk said he was "flabbergasted," and a number of policemen, including the IAD director, were demoted in the wake of the report.

Critics also argue that through internal police review procedures, the Mayor has a means of control which is not clearly visible to the public. They point out that the Superintendent of Police has absolute authority in disciplinary matters. He can overrule the recommendations of the reviewing panel, and the Police Board cannot consider a case without his approval. The Superintendent in turn holds office at the pleasure of the Mayor. This means, the critics charge, that the Mayor has ultimate power to decide the outcome of any IAD investigation; and, they contend the investigation of the Black Panther raid was a case in point. Their most charitable interpretation is that the IAD instinctively knew the finding Mayor Daley wanted it to reach in that politically charged affair.

The question of Mayor Daley's influence in police matters poses a more fundamental issue: namely, the acceptability of active mayoralty involvement in the police jurisdiction. As we observed in New York City, Commissioners and patrolmen alike have vigorously resisted mayoralty leadership. And after the Philadelphia election of 1967, Mayor Tate openly espoused the virtues of police independence. In Chicago, there is no evidence of police resistance to Daley's leadership. Superintendent James B. Conlisk, Jr. has said that Daley has given him only one order, to run a first-rate police department. In an interview, however, Conlisk was asked: "Well, whether or not he gives you a direct order, you know how he thinks, don't you—and you're responsive to that, aren't you?" "Oh sure, I'm responsive," the Superintendent replied. "I think police departments must be responsive to civil authority because the civil authority represents the people of the community. And we are totally responsive to the people of the community." [40]

A matter that has not been fully resolved is whether the previous Superintendent, O.W. Wilson, would have responded in the same manner as Conlisk. Wilson, after all, was called in by the Mayor as a reformer who could clean up the Police Department and give it a new professional image after a major police scandal. Any answer to this query represents mere speculation, but in his book *Boss,* Mike Royko observes that after the Martin Luther King demonstrations in the Summer of 1966, Daley wanted a new tough approach. Royko continues:

> Wilson said he retired because he was sixty–seven and wanted to relax. But for a long time rumors persisted that he had been deftly eased out by Daley, who wanted someone who would follow his get–tough orders. In Wilson's replacement, James Conlisk, Daley had such a man. Conlisk's father had been a friend of Daley's, and was one of the seven aged, politically heavy, assistant superintendents who ran the Police Department in the pre–Wilson days. The younger Conlisk, while an able administrator, had none of Wilson's personal stature and independence. He would say "yes sir" when Daley told him what to do.[41]

NOTES

1. *Police and Public, A Critique and A Program,* Final Report of the Citizens' Committee to Study Police–Community Relations in the City of Chicago to Mayor Richard J. Daley, May 22, 1967, p. 24.
2. *The Chicago Tribune,* August 26, 1966.
3. *Ibid.,* August 6, 1968.
4. The Albert J. Reiss study covered eight slum precincts in Washington, Boston and Chicago as reported in *The New York Times,* July 5, 1968.
5. "Dissent and Disorder," A Report to the Citizens of Chicago on the April 27 Peace Parade, Illinois Division of the American Civil Liberties Union, August 1, 1968, p. 30.
6. See the reprint in the *Chicago Tribune,* September 7, 1968.
7. *Ibid.*
8. *Ibid.*
9. National Commission on the Causes and Prevention of Violence, *Rights in Conflict,* (The Walker Report), (New York: Bantam Books, 1968), p. xvi.
10. *Ibid.,* p. 1.
11. *Ibid.,* p. 3.
12. *Ibid.,* p. 11.
13. *The New York Times,* March 21, 1969.
14. *The New York Times,* August 25, 1971.
15. *Chicago Daily News,* March 17, 1972.
16. *Ibid.*

17. *Ibid.*
18. *The Chicago Tribune,* October 27, 1972.
19. *The New York Times,* February 7, 1966.
20. *Ibid.,* August 11, 1967.
21. See Joseph D. Lohman and Gordon E. Misner, *The Police and the Community,* Vol. 2, A Report of a Research Study Submitted to the President's Commission on Law Enforcement and Administration of Justice (Washington, D.C.: U.S. Government Printing Office, October, 1966).
22. *The Philadelphia Inquirer,* January 2, 1968.
23. *The Philadelphia Bulletin,* April 21, 1969.
24. *The New York Times,* December 13, 1967.
25. Francis W.H. Adams, *The New York Times,* February 17, 1966.
26. *The New York Times,* February 22, 1966.
27. *Ibid.,* December 11, 1967.
28. *Ibid.*
29. *Ibid.*
30. *Ibid.,* December 13, 1967.
31. *Ibid.,* August 13, 1968.
32. *Ibid.,* August 14, 1968.
33. Lohman and Misner, *The Police and the Community,* op. cit., p. 37.
34. *Ibid.,* p. 37.
35. *First Annual Report of the Police Review Board of the City Philadelphia* (Philadelphia Police Review Board), September, 1959, p. 1. (Mimeographed.)
36. *The Philadelphia Inquirer,* March 29, 1967.
37. *The Philadelphia Bulletin,* July 11, 1969.
38. *Ibid.,* December 28, 1969.
39. Testimony of Virgil Penn, Recording Secretary of the Fraternal Order of the Police in Philadelphia. Samuel Lubell confirms the importance of the Tate strategy in his data on racial polarization in Philadelphia in *The Hidden Crisis in American Politics* (New York: W.W. Norton and Co., 1970), pp. 92–5.
40. *The Chicago Sun-Times,* December 2, 1970.
41. Mike Royko, *Boss: Richard J. Daley of Chicago* (New York: E.P. Dutton & Co., 1971), p. 165.

Chapter Four

The Politics of Law and Order

Widespread anxiety over public protests, violence, and crime, particularly in our big cities, has placed a heavy burden on the police. Because they are the most visible part of the law enforcement process, the public has presumed great expectations about what the police can do in preserving order and social stability. Yet, as the Task Force Report on the Police explains, the ability of the police to achieve these objectives is limited. "The police did not create and cannot resolve the social conditions that stimulate crime. They did not start and cannot stop the social changes that are taking place in America. They do not enact the laws that they are required to enforce, nor do they dispose of the criminals they arrest."[1]

The sense of frustration that comes from the contradictions of their daily work has, in many instances, encouraged the police to enter the political arena. There they seek to influence affairs which have traditionally been considered outside of their jurisdiction. One special target has been the criminal laws and judicial procedures which appear to them to "coddle criminals" and to sanction "permissiveness." How successful they are in effecting themselves in our three sample cities is something that we shall now consider.

Philadelphia

If the traditional expectation is that it is the Mayor, like the President, who is protector of the public peace, then Philadelphia appears to be something of an exception. Table 4–1 shows the strong leadership which has been exercised in that city by the Police Commissioner; more leadership, as measured by the number of successes, than the Mayor or anyone else. All this was achieved by Frank Rizzo who served as Commissioner from 1967 to 1971.

Shortly after assuming Philadelphia's top police post in May of 1967, Rizzo gave clear indication of how he intended to carry out the law. Promising to deal quickly and sternly with any disturbances that would arise during the coming "long, hot summer," he explained that he considered himself "a tough disciplinarian." "If one of these outside agitators comes in (to Philadelphia), he'll be taken on and taken on quickly. . . . And he may be very sorry he came to Philadelphia."[2] Rizzo also expressed disappointment with the United States Supreme Court for having made the policeman's job tougher. "Someone, someplace is going to have to reconsider," he said. "I think we have gone too far."[3]

Toward the middle of June, a series of racial incidences and police skirmishes in South Philadelphia indicated that the anticipated long, hot summer had arrived. A court injunction, which forbade a local NAACP leader from speaking in a black residential area, seemed to add to the rising neighborhood tensions. Fearful of an eruption similar to the violence that had spread to other cities in the country, Mayor James Tate issued a proclamation on July 27 placing the city in a state of "limited emergency." The prime effect of this was to mobilize the city's seven thousand-man police force to administer a ban on gatherings of twelve or more persons.

Tate's strategy was to impose a swift and firm response to avoid the chaos that had developed in Newark and Detroit. But his actions here had broader implications, for the administration's show of force seemed to be effective at the very time that Tate was running for reelection. The Mayor continued to stress his commander-in-chief role all through the summer: he extended over-time police patrols beyond the two weeks originally specified for his declared "emergency"; and he pushed through the city council seven special ordinances which would assist city authorities in dealing with any future civil disorder. For example, the Mayor was formerly authorized to declare a state of unlimited emergency banning outdoor gatherings, Molotov cocktails were outlawed, and new regulations were imposed on the distribution and use of guns, ammunition and explosives. Tate was able to make full use of these powers again in the Spring of 1968 to quell disturbances after the assassination of the Reverend Martin Luther King.

Mayor Tate's leadership during this period was rewarded by an unexpected victory at the polls in November of 1967. But it also became clear that Tate could not have succeeded without the strong support of Commissioner Rizzo and the police. Where the Republican candidate for Mayor, Arlen Specter, indicated that he might not keep Rizzo if elected, Tate heaped the highest praise on his loyal public servant. Speaking of him at a testimonial, Tate expounded: "Not only Philadelphia, but the whole Nation recognizes his foresight, understanding, courage, and determination. What you are doing here tonight in honoring him, mirrors the trust the community places in him." [4]

In a city of mounting racial tensions, such testimony oft repeated could only add to the controversy surrounding Rizzo. Soon after the Fall elections, Rizzo became even more controversial in his handling of a student "black power" demonstration outside the School Administration Building. The Commissioner alleged that two policemen were on the ground grappling with demonstrators when he waved his nightstick at a formation of more than one hundred officers and commandered them to go to the rescue. During the violent clashes that followed, at least twenty persons were injured including five policemen, and fifty-seven persons were arrested. Former Mayor Richardson Dilworth, now President of the Board of Education, argued that it was police action which triggered the violence and he decried the fact that the police had acted without consulting school authorities.

Mayor Tate's reaction was to give full support to the police. "The Board (of Education) has not only failed to curb Black Power activities in the schools," the Mayor said, "but it has also failed to keep in touch with the police." [5] Thereafter, in virtually every public confrontation, the Mayor continued to give strong backing to Rizzo. So, too, was support forthcoming from the local chapter of the Fraternal Order of the Police.

For the most part, Rizzo's impressive record of victories during his reign as Commissioner was achieved in battles with civil liberties groups and spokesmen for Philadelphia's black population. Law suits against Rizzo and the police, charging denial of free speech and assembly during the November 17 student demonstrations were to no avail. To preserve order in the schools, the Commissioner succeeded in assigning police to the public schools over the opposition of the school board. The Commissioner, moreover, soon established the practice of personally requesting legislation from the city council. One ordinance which was passed, banned the open display in streets or meeting-places of any weapon with a cutting edge (reportedly Rizzo was anticipating a Black Power convention in the city whose participants sometimes carry long ceremonial knives). Another ordinance requested by Rizzo empowered the police to enter colleges and universities on evidence of persons bearing arms.

The only instance of disharmony on law and order matters between the Mayor and the Commissioner was when Rizzo requisitioned two tank-like riot control vehicles to be used by the police. Following a public outcry over "tanks in our streets" from the leaders of black organizations, Tate was forced to cancel the order. Another defeat that Rizzo experienced together with the

Table 4-1. Law and Order Leaders

| | New York City | | Philadelphia | | Chicago | |
	Successes	Defeats	Successes	Defeats	Successes	Defeats
Mayor	4	–	5	1	16	–
Cmnr./Supt.	4	–	7	2	1	2
Police officers/Dept.	–	–	1	–	2	4
Policemen's assns.	2	4	–	–	–	–
Others	9	**	6	**	6	**
Total successes*	19	**	19	**	25	**

*Number of successes do not equal the total number of decisions as more than one person can be attributed with having been successful in a particular decision.

**Not estimated.

Mayor and District Attorney Specter, was over a program urged upon the city's judiciary to meet the problems of gang war and criminal repeaters. The judges considered proposals of maximum sentences, preventive detention and the elimination of bail under certain circumstances as being unduly harsh and in violation of legal standards.

But in spite of these two setbacks, Commissioner Rizzo continued to build his popularity before the general citizenry. As he was fond of explaining, if the city of Philadelphia lacked proper security during periods of unrest or if criminal repeaters were free to roam in the streets, it was not his fault; rather, it was the fault of the "sob-sisters" who didn't understand crime control.

Chicago

In Chicago, as Table 4-1 shows, it is the Mayor who is clearly ascendant in the role of protector of the public peace. The data also reveal the degree to which Chicago has been plagued by violence. On five separate occasions during this four year period, Mayor Daley was forced to mobilize the Chicago police and to seek the assistance of the Illinois National Guard; and on two occasions in 1968, he requested and received the support of federal troops.

In question during this time are not only the root-causes of the social turmoil which took place, but also the quality of response by the city fathers. The day after the assassination of the Reverend Martin Luther King, disorder broke out in many cities throughout the United States. But it was Mayor Richard Daley who provoked the most attention when he ordered city policemen to "shoot to kill" arsonists, and to "shoot to maim or cripple" looters so they could be detained. He also suggested that chemical mace be used in detaining children found looting. In obvious anger, Daley explained at a press conference that he thought orders to shoot arsonists and looters were in effect when rioting began in the city on April 5.

Spurred by rumors that he was about to lose his job, Police Superintendent James B. Conlisk reacted quickly to the Mayor's commands. This was in spite of the fact that they seemed to conflict with police order 67-14 which limits the use of firearms by police in crowds. A veteran detective explained, "(i)f we fire on looters in a riot, you'd have bullets flying all over the place and 67-14 would go out the window."[6] However, Joseph J. LeFevour, President of the Chicago chapter of the Fraternal Order of Police, apparently had no doubts. He sent a telegram to Daley praising him for what he called the Mayor's "positive position."[7] (After a few days when the riots were ending, Daley attempted to qualify his statement by speaking of the need to use minimum force. But he never actually rescinded his orders.)

According to the Walker Commission, Mayor Daley's angry words in April set a tone which were at least partly responsible for the violent episodes which followed a few months later at the Democratic National Convention. Anticipating trouble from antiwar protestors who would be arriving from all parts of the country, and fearful of what black power groups could do, Daley and the Police Department planned a strong show of military force. By the time the convention began, massive security arrangements had been completed.

> Chicago's twelve thousand policemen had been put on twelve-hour shifts; five thousand Illinois national guardsmen had been mobilized and were standing by near the downtown area; six thousand specially trained army troops were flown in and were in combat readiness at the Glenview Naval Air Station, just north of the city; several hundred state and county lawmen were on call; and the largest number of secret service agents ever used at a political convention were in Chicago. Including the private security workers hired for the Amphitheatre, a defense force of at least twenty-five thousand was in Chicago.[8]

Violence began on August 24 when the city refused permission to demonstrators to use Lincoln Park after 11 p.m. It continued for the next six days on the streets of Chicago and by the time it ended, a total of 668 persons had been arrested. Estimates of injuries sustained by civilians place the number at over a thousand. Police Department records reported a total of 192 policemen injured.

In a very real sense, then, Mayor Daley was the commander-in-chief of his city. And, as to be expected in the proper performance of this role, he has unflinchingly defended his troops from all forms of criticism, whatever the source. To counter television monitoring of the street attacks during the Convention, he agreed to be interviewed by Walter Cronkite of CBS. If the police were acting tough, it was for good reason he explained. "There were reports and intelligence on my desk that certain people planned to assassinate the three contenders for the presidency; that certain people planned to assassinate many of the leaders, including myself. So I took the necessary precautions."[9] (Mike Royko reports in his book that there was never any follow-up to ascertain the verity of these claims.) Within a week after the Convention concluded, Daley's staff produced an "official" report called "The Strategy of Confrontation." It repeated the Mayor's claim of expected assassinations and put the blame for the disorders squarely on the demonstrators and the press.[10] For good measure, Mayor Daley also hired a television producer to create a TV special of the city's side of the controversy.

In the interludes between riots and demonstrations, Mayor Daley prepared for trouble in other ways. In March of 1968, he induced the City Council to place new restrictions on picketing and demonstrations near schools and churches. (Labor disputes were exempted.) To meet challenges in the courts, ordinances defining disorderly conduct and resisting arrest were clarified. With the Council's cooperation, Daley also succeeded in amending the city code so as to allow policemen to stop and frisk persons who arouse suspicion.

Of some significance is the fact that in asserting his "law and order" leadership, Daley received no rebuffs—at least none that could be seen in the public record. Rebuffs were reserved, rather, for the Police Department and the Superintendent of Police. In such instances, it was federal court findings of law enforcement overreach on questions of the proper use of search warrants, interference with newsgathering, and the regulation of public demonstrations that served to limit police action.

New York City

Mayor Daley's "shoot to kill" and "shoot to maim" order of April 1968 in Chicago provoked wide national controversy. Among the many persons to react was John V. Lindsay, Mayor of New York City. Citing his experience as Vice Chairman of the National Advisory Commission on Civil Disorders (the Kerner Commission), Lindsay articulated a very different philosophy. "We happen to think that protection of life, particularly innocent life, is more important than protecting property or anything else. . . . We are not going to turn disorder into chaos through the unprincipled use of armed force." [11]

Here, then, is the criteria by which Lindsay and his Police Commissioner, Howard Leary, were to act on questions of law and order during the period 1966 to 1969. To assure proper arrest and judicial procedures during civil disturbances, Lindsay established the Committee on Administration of Criminal Justice Under Emergency Conditions. Composed of the Police Commissioner, the district attorneys of the five boroughs, representatives from the bar associations, Deputy Mayor Robert W. Sweet and Corporation Counsel J. Lee Rankin, the Committee was instructed to review and revise statutes and procedures to accomplish the following: insure the arrest and prosecution of those who riot or incite to riot; provide prompt arraignment and judicial hearings under conditions that would not aggravate grievances in a disturbed area; provide counsel for those who need legal service and insure that bail and release procedures protect individual rights; provide adequate and accessible detention facilities for those arrested. A Courts Committee on Civil Disorders was also created to perform a parallel function for the judicial branch. Such arrangements, it was pointed out, were in accordance with the comprehensive recommendations of the Kerner Commission Report on Civil Disorders.

The disturbances which erupted in Harlem and Bedford–Stuyvesant following the assassination of Dr. Martin Luther King in the Spring of 1968 prompted Mayor Lindsay to augment his authority as commander–in–chief. But even here, in seeking extraordinary powers of civil control during emergencies, Lindsay's model was the Kerner Commission Report. As referred to, the Report states:

> Civil disorders are fundamental governmental problems, not simply police matters. As the chief elected official, the mayor must take ultimate responsibility for all governmental action in time of disorder. To make this meaningful, he must have the corresponding authority and control. He must become fully involved in disorder planning and operations. . . . In some cities, mayors have taken the view that disorders were fundamentally police powers. This represents a failure to accept a fundamental responsibility.[12]

Accordingly, Lindsay requested and received from the City Council new powers to declare a state of emergency for up to fifteen days, to impose curfews, to prohibit pedestrian and vehicular traffic, to ban the sale of alcoholic beverages and to close places of public assembly. The Mayor was authorized to invoke these powers if and when he believes there is a "clear and present danger" of riot or public disorder.

Following Lindsay's lead, Police Commissioner Howard Leary urged changes in arraignment procedures which would reduce delays. The purpose was to avoid charges of coerced confessions during interim waits in police precinct cells. Among the reforms instituted were twenty–four hour criminal court arraignment centers in each borough for major crimes and provision for release with a summons for persons arrested for minor offenses. Under Lindsay's goadings, furthermore, the Committee on Administration of Criminal Justice Under Emergency Conditions prepared "disorder contingency plans" which provided for the quick arraignment of rioters and structured a system of operations which would separate arrested rioters from regular prisoners.

But if Lindsay and Leary believed they were working out a useful set of strategies to cope with crime and disorder, there were others in the City of New York who thought differently. An allegation heard again and again was that the Lindsay administration was soft on crime and encouraged permissiveness. What gave special significance to this charge is that the organized policemen were the most outspoken group to proffer it.

The first taste of this occurred during antidraft demonstrations in December of 1967. As discussed in the previous chapter, Mayor Lindsay instructed two of his aides—Barry Gottehrer and Sid Davidoff—to walk along with the demonstrators and try to act as a communication link between them and the police. But the leaders of the Patrolmen's Benevolent Association took a dim view of this and demanded that the two assistants resign because of their interference with police operations. In his rebuttal, Lindsay made it clear that he is commander-in-chief of the city just as the President of the United States is commander-in-chief of the nation. Therefore, he insisted, it was his responsibility to set policy on such matters.

Charges of "coddling" and "Lindsay intervention" continued during the Spring and Summer of 1968. There were public outcries over the apparent low profile of police in black districts after the assassination of Martin Luther King, Jr., and the belief that they were allowing looters to operate without interference. While there was some concern at the time that not enough policemen were available to exercise effective control, it seemed clear that a decision had been made to let the disorder run its course in an effort to avoid an escalation in rioting. Criticism of Lindsay intensified in July of 1968 when some fifteen hundred Harlem youths demonstrated at City Hall against cutbacks in summer job programs. When the protest became violent, the police at first did little more than watch. Lending support to the growing chorus of criticism were City Controller Mario A. Procaccino and City Council President Frank D. O'Connor, the second and third ranking office holders in the city.

Matters reached a peak in mid-August when the head of the Patrolmen's Benevolent Association, John J. Cassesse attempted to issue his own "get tough" instructions to the organization's twenty-nine thousand members. "In the last two and a half years we've followed a policy of restraint that emanated from City Hall—a policy of turning the other cheek and not getting involved," said Cassesse during a news conference. "Now, I say, let's try the other side of the coin."[13] The P.B.A. leader stated that later in the week he would issue guidelines to his men calling for complete law enforcement "regardless of what orders we may get from any superior officer."[14] Cassesse recognized that the new policy would bring him into "direct conflict" with City Hall. But as we previously noted, when Commissioner Leary warned of disciplinary action, Cassesse in effect backed down—the Patrolmen's Benevolent Association sent its members excerpts from the Police Department's rules and state law emphasizing their duty to obey only the lawful orders of superiors in the Department.

A related issue which crystallized at about the same time grew out of a complaint against Criminal Court Judge John F. Furey by a dissident group of policemen. Known as the Law Enforcement Group (L.E.G.), this faction within the Patrolmen's Benevolent Association circulated a petition which demanded that the P.B.A. work for the removal of Judge Furey because he was alleged to have permitted disorderly conduct in his court during the arraignment of two members of the Black Panther organization. Though the judge denied the charges, L.E.G. persisted in its demand and was soon incorporating new ones. As amended, the petition called for the following: a grand jury investigation of "coddling" of criminal suspects; the abolition of the Police Department's Civilian Complaint Review Board (the successor to the old civilian controlled review board); contact and support of United States Senators "who are trying to prevent another Warren Court" (an apparent reference to opponents of the naming of Abe Fortas as Chief Justice of the Supreme Court); work for the raising of physical and mental entrance requirements for the Police Department. These were necessary, the group argued, to "protect the life and welfare of police officers and to seek all the assistance possible to enable them to vigorously enforce the laws of this state."[15] According to press reports, at least six thousand New York policemen signed the petition.

On September 4, 1968, an incident took place which exacerbated an already tense situation. During a preliminary hearing for three Black Panthers accused of assaulting a policeman, a group of approximately one hundred–fifty white men—many of them out–of–uniform and off–duty policemen—assaulted a small group of Panther sympathizers. The attack in which three blacks were hurt, took place on the sixth floor of the Brooklyn Criminal Court building. Reacting quickly, Commissioner Leary sent a message the very next day to all police commands in which he warned members of the police force that the "department will not tolerate any unlawful actions on the part of individual police officers on or off duty, and when the situation warrants, violators will be arrested."[16] The remainder of the message read like an exercise in constitutional law:

> The Constitution of the United States and the State of New York and the laws adopted thereunder guarantee to every person equal protection under the law.
>
> Among the basic freedoms guaranteed is the right to peaceable assembly and protest. Such protests and assemblies, however, must take into consideration the rights of others including the right of a fair trial. Therefore, demonstrations which disrupt the sanctity of the courthouse and are designed to intimidate the court are not legitimate exercises of such a constitutional right. Every person must be guaranteed a fair and impartial trial. The court and witnesses must be free of coercion and harassment so that all the facts are fairly presented through the proper tribunal.
>
> It is the duty of the members of the department to bring violators before the court so that society, by its duly constituted machinery, can administer justice under the law.

The police officer is a public officer who has taken an oath to uphold the laws of the land. When police officers violate the rights of others, a most grave situation results—public confidence in law is weakened and respect for authority is undermined.[17]

Circumstantial evidence which appeared to show that members of L.E.G. were involved in the assault made this event appear even more ominous. Though leaders of the group denied any role, it had become clear to the P.B.A. leadership that such militancy posed a threat which had to be dealt with. In a noisy closed-door session during their annual meeting in the Catskills of upstate New York, P.B.A. delegates approved a resolution condemning any group or person bringing discredit on the New York Police Department through "unlawful, antisocial or violent acts." Though the resolution did not directly link the Law Enforcement Group with such acts, it said that the organization had attempted to usurp the powers of the P.B.A. and thereby "threatened to gravely damage the reputation, impair the community relations and reduce the ability of the Patrolmen's Benevolent Association to represent its members effectively."[18] In light of this response, the leaders of L.E.G. had no choice but to assume that its petition was dead.

Though L.E.G. had evidently lost the skirmish, some observers noted that it had succeeded at least in prodding the P.B.A. toward a more aggressive posture in behalf of policemen's interests. Taking time off from the pressure of events surrounding him, Commissioner Leary contemplated the reasons for the emergence of a militant right wing in the New York Police Department. "They are reflecting the community," he said. "I think what we have here is verbal expression and demonstration by a small group of policemen—which might reflect a greater number—as to their concern for adherence to the laws of the land. This shouldn't surprise us. We have almost 30,000 policemen who live in communities and they speak to people and get more or less the same views from these contacts."[19]

NOTES

1. President's Commission on Law Enforcement and Administration of Justice, *Task Force Report: The Police, op. cit.,* p. 1.
2. *The Philadelphia Inquirer,* May 22, 1967.
3. *Ibid.*
4. *The Philadelphia Inquirer,* October 1, 1967.
5. *Ibid.,* November 19, 1967.
6. *The Chicago Tribune,* April 16, 1968.
7. *Ibid.*
8. Mike Royko, *op. cit.,* p. 182.

9. *Ibid.*, p. 191.
10. See the discussion of this report in Chapter 3.
11. *The New York Times*, April 17, 1968.
12. U.S. Riot Commission, *Report of the National Advisory Commission on Civil Disorders* (New York: Bantam Books, 1968), p. 333.
13. *The New York Times*, August 13, 1968.
14. *Ibid.*
15. *Ibid.*, August 20, 1968.
16. *Ibid.*, September 6, 1968.
17. *Ibid.*
18. *Ibid.*, September 13, 1968.
19. *Ibid.*, September 11, 1968.

Chapter Five

Police and Community

Since the violent confrontations of the 1960's, there has been much open discussion about the need to strengthen police-community relations. For the most part, proposals have centered on police-citizen contacts and the ways and means of reducing the tensions and hostility which can result from such contacts.[1] Posed this way, the subject tends to be rather narrowly defined as a sociological problem in intergroup relations. To broaden the focus, it is necessary to view police-community relations as a power phenomenon. This is to say that the police may in some instances be quite willing to expand their community role for purposes of asserting influence and control. At the same time, there may be those who resist such efforts because they fear police power.

As a way of testing this out, Table 5-1 presents us with a profile view of police-community decision making in our three sample cities. The question treated here is: who successfully initiates and who successfully vetoes proposals which structure police involvement and accessibility to other groups and jurisdictions? We are also interested in examining the proposals themselves as well as the circumstances which surround them. This will help in determining whether police-community relations programs in any way affected the power stakes of either the police or other key participants. Before proceeding to our analysis, we should note that temporary and experimental programs of limited scope are not considered here; rather, we treat only those issues which are of broad community significance. (Consult Appendices A, B, and C for specific case references.)

Philadelphia

During the turbulence of the 1960's, Philadelphia was one of the first major cities in the United States to have a riot. In August of 1964, three days of looting and turmoil in the North Central wards resulted in two deaths,

63

Table 5-1. Police and Community: Leaders

	New York City		Philadelphia		Chicago	
	Successes	Defeats	Successes	Defeats	Successes	Defeats
Mayor	2	1	3	—	—	—
Cmnr./Supt.	4	—	5	—	2	—
Police officers/Dept.	1	—	2	—	1	—
Policemen's assns.	2	2	3	—	—	—
Others	3	**	6	**	5	**
Total successes*	12		19		8	

*Number of successes do not equal the total number of decisions as more than one person can be attributed with having been successful in a particular decision.

**Not estimated.

339 persons wounded (239 were black residents and 100 were police and constables), and 308 persons arrested. Total property damage was estimated at three million dollars.

In the aftermath, it was anticipated that the city could learn from this tragic experience and build anew. "Responsible community involvement," after all, had been something of a tradition in the "city of brotherly love." To prove the point, residents could cite the fact that Philadelphia had initiated formal police-community programs earlier than any other large city. Lending their support to such programs, ranking administrators in the Police Department attested to the importance of police-community relations. For example, former Police Commissioner Howard Leary discussed the subject in the following way:

> We (the police) simply have to change . . . in order to relate to the community as it wants us to. We must make the changes which the community wants us to make. And the only way we can do this is through a closer relationship of the Police Department to the community at large.[2]

By way of elaboration, Leary stressed the importance of finding ways in which citizens could be given a participatory role in the Police Department because, as he explained, the police desperately need an infusion of civilian attitudes.

His successor, Commissioner Edward J. Bell, reflected a similar point of view as expressed in a letter to the North City Congress. (In 1966, the North City Congress received a federal grant to educate policemen and citizens on the subject of police community relations.)

> The bringing together of police in the local districts and the residents of the communities for a common education and understanding of each others problems and activities should be of great value. It should help to reduce the hostility and tensions that exist in some communities at this time.[3]

Bell, however, did not last too long—a mere six months—and the appointment of Frank Rizzo in May of 1967 heralded in a new and more dynamic view of the role of the police in the community. If, as we've seen, ranking law officers could profess concern over how the police must strive to accommodate the community, the new perspective now becomes one of how the community must accommodate the police. The data in Table 5-1 shows the extent to which Commissioner Rizzo (all scoring under "Commissioner" is attributable to Rizzo), police officers and leaders of the Fraternal Order of Police were able to assert themselves in community affairs. More importantly, the case material reveals how these participants worked together to establish police influence in sectors not ordinarily within the police orbit.

The event which best symbolizes the new attitude in Philadelphia is what observors have called "the big bust" of November 17, 1967. On that day, as we related in Chapter 3, Commissioner Rizzo personally led his policemen into a crowd of some thirty-five hundred student "black power" protestors outside the Board of Education. A number of injuries resulted and School Board President Richardson Dilworth felt compelled to criticize the police action as irresponsible. Other groups and organizations quickly got into the act. While some six hundred persons, mostly white, picketed City Hall with signs which denounced the Police Commissioner, the Philadelphia-based National Association for the Advancement of Colored People demanded the immediate dismissal of Rizzo. Another black group announced it would lead a boycott of center city stores until Rizzo was replaced; and a poverty organization, Community Legal Services, Inc., filed a suit demanding Rizzo's ouster.

In the face of this opposition, Rizzo backers rallied to defend "effective law enforcement." Included among them were voters in South Philadelphia and the Northeast who were uneasy over rising racial tensions and who had supported Mayor Tate in the recent election. Additional support came from the Fraternal Order of Police and various veterans' groups. Mayor Tate showed whose side he was on by openly calling Rizzo "the best law enforcement officer in the land." [4]

In the end, under the Mayor's goadings, it was Dilworth and his supporters who had to back down. Emerging from a meeting on November 30, the Mayor and the School Board President proclaimed "a new era of good relationship" between city and school officials. A series of contractual agreements was announced between the City and the School Board making for closer working relations in the field of police, recreation, health and planning in fiscal matters. In addition, it was agreed that there would be at least one policeman in every city school during class hours—a total of twenty policemen in all. As a sidelight, the Mayor also disclosed that he had decided to ignore the suggestion that the Board be billed one million dollars which was spent by the city to pay police for working twelve-hour shifts in the wake of the student disturbance.

But racial tensions in the schools would not be quelled. When, the uneasy truce between black and white high school students erupted into a series of clashes in October of 1968, the issue of security in the public schools exploded once again. Rizzo claimed that trouble could have been avoided entirely if a previous request to establish sufficient police control in the schools had not been watered down. Reacting to this, Mayor Tate recommended that the Police Department take over school security. But Dilworth and other Board members resisted the idea of a "school unit" in the Police Department on the grounds that this would turn the public schools into little police states. They claimed that Rizzo wanted eighty to one hundred uniformed guards on patrol under his control. It was also alleged that the Commissioner wanted picture-bearing identification cards issued to all students and a veto over outside speakers coming into the schools. In an angry confrontation on November 18, according to Board members, Rizzo gave notice that he had "dossiers" on some of the resisting school leaders.

When the issue was finally resolved two days later, it was clear that Rizzo had achieved at least a partial victory: twenty additional policemen would be assigned to troubled schools though they would be under the control of the principals. The Board also abandoned its plan to hire its own security guards. In his assessment of the settlement, Rizzo explained that the presence of uniformed policemen in the schools would not only deter troublemakers but would help to establish a better rapport between students and police officers.

After this experience with the Board of Education, Commissioner Rizzo turned his attention to other sectors. In May of 1969, he requested an ordinance from the City Council banning the carrying of weapons on campuses and other "public and private grounds" excluding homes. In addition, the proposed law would empower the police for the first time to enter a campus or building uninvited on evidence that demonstrators or potential troublemakers are bearing arms. Said Rizzo: "I am going to assure all the people of this city that we are not going to permit anyone to bear arms on the campusses of our colleges and universities. We are not going to permit situations which have occurred on campuses all over the country. This will not be tolerated in Philadelphia." [5] City Council President Paul D'Ortona agreed and blamed "weaklings" who direct our educational institutions for making such legislation necessary.

But various heads of institutions such as churches and libraries as well as schools did not quite see it that way; and university presidents in Philadelphia took a dim view of the implications of unexpected police investigations on campus. Confronted with a vocal opposition, Rizzo compromised. As finally passed on July 9, the ordinance addressed itself only to demonstrations in the city's schools and on campuses of colleges and universities; in addition, the police would have to ask permission before entering such places in search of weapons. Though the Commissioner got less than he originally asked for, it was also clear that through skillful bargaining, he and the Police Department came away with more than they had before.

At about the same time that this proposal was being argued, another issue was in the making. On June 3, 1969, John J. Harrington and other ranking officials of the national Fraternal Order of Police visited Attorney General

John Mitchell in Washington, D.C. Their purpose was to complain about the use of federal funds for the hiring of lawyers to represent poor people with grievances against the police. Harrington referred specifically to a federal grand jury investigation against six Philadelphia policemen where lawyers, hired through the Neighborhood Legal Services program of the Office of Economic Opportunity, helped bring charges of police brutality. There were "well over a hundred" similar cases across the country he said.[6] Harrington and his entourage then gave the Attorney General a petition signed by 100,000 FOP members and 550,000 citizens seeking reversal of Supreme Court decisions deemed to favor lawbreakers while placing "an unnecessary and unfair burden" on policemen.

A few days later, while testifying before the Public Safety Committee of the Philadelphia City Council, Commissioner Rizzo seemingly picked up the cue and began an attack on the United Fund for supporting agencies that hire lawyers "to take us on." "If this doesn't stop" he continued, "there will not be another penny contributed to the United Fund."[7] Later, the Commissioner explained that while he had not mentioned the organization before the committee, he was referring to the Legal Aid Society "and several others." He said he believed in "legal aid for the underprivileged and the poor and police support this, but when it's used by the militant groups, we object."[8]

Rizzo's reference to the Legal Aid Society was puzzling to the officers of this organization because the Society handles only civil cases. Nor was it involved in the furor caused in 1967 by an action to oust Rizzo, first by Community Legal Services and later by individual lawyers. The next day, Rizzo made another charge against the United Fund accusing the agency of giving financial support to persons who are not poor and who could afford to pay lawyers from out of their own pockets. This time he did not mention any specific names or cases. Unexpectedly caught in public controversy, the United Fund denied that it supported agencies that harass the police. The United Fund also released a statement warning that unjustified attacks against it constituted an assault against the broad spectrum of services provided by its agencies.

On June 29, Fraternal Order of Police President John Harrington joined the fray when he disclosed the results of police undercover work. Three patrolmen, he said, in civilian clothing—two black and one white—approached the Legal Aid Society with their heads bandaged and complained that they had been beaten by policemen. Instead of calling the incident to the attention of District Attorney Specter or Commissioner Rizzo, Harrington said, the three were sent to the Civil Liberties Union, Community Legal Services, Inc., and Philadelphians for Equal Justice. These were the organizations which were attacked by Harrington and Rizzo for past conflicts with police and which,

Harrington declared, "have us fed up with the United Fund and their strongarm methods."[9] In expressing his support of Harrington, Rizzo declared, "We need no vehicle to go to the poor. And as long as the Legal Aid Society continues to refer people to agencies other than the Police Department without giving us the opportunity to review the situation, I see no reason why policemen have to help."[10]

Harrington and Rizzo also outlined grievances that centered on the role played by the Fellowship Commission, an old-time reform organization that had been arguing for the reinstatement of the Police Advisory Board. They contended that there was an "association" between the Commission and the United Fund, "indirectly and through splinter groups." Robert W. Reifsnyder, United Fund executive director, denied these allegations and warned that inaccurate statements could imperil the organization's yearly campaign to raise necessary funds. Maurice B. Fagan, executive director of the Fellowship Commission, accused Harrington of going off "half cocked without the facts" and said the Commission "has never taken a dime from the United Fund or the Federal Government in its 28-year history."[11] He explained that the organization is independently financed through the efforts of its seven thousand members, including representatives of corporations and church groups throughout the city. But in spite of these denials, the F.O.P. membership unanimously passed a resolution to support its leader by refusing to make its usual contributions to the United Fund.

Caught by surprise, Mayor Tate's response was to offer to mediate the dispute though he agreed that "it is up to the organizations to prove that they are not harassing the police."[12] Applying pressure over the following three weeks, the Mayor succeeded in coaxing an "official" reconciliation between the disputants. In announcing the settlement on July 25, Commissioner Rizzo said that the Legal Aid Society's procedure for handling police complaints would be to first file a statement with him. If the complainant did not agree with the disposition, he could go back to the Society. The Society then would tell him that police cases were not in its jurisdiction and it would not volunteer names of other legal groups that could take up the cases. However, if the complainant asked for another law group that might take his case, the Society could then refer him. In light of the agreement, Rizzo said he would ask the men in his department to reconsider their request to cancel paycheck deductions for the United Fund.

After tempers had cooled, United Fund insisted that it had not been compelled to change its practices at all. But even if this were true, the police establishment had nevertheless successfully forged an instrument with which it could confront other community groups. Henceforth, organizations which worked in behalf of persons accused of crime would be on the defensive.

It is interesting to note that a similar challenge had been carried out two years earlier when John J. Harrington brought formal charges that Philadelphia's General Hospital medical staff was incompetent and displayed negligence when administering medical aid to policemen. A special committee created by the City Council to investigate the charges heard witness after witness testify about incidents of malpractice. Harrington himself told the story of how physicians at the hospital started a brain operation on a policeman only to discover that they had the wrong patient. A few months later, in January of 1968, Mayor Tate reorganized the hospital's administration. Among four new appointees to the Board of Trustees were John Harrington, President of the Fraternal Order of Police and Raymond Hemmert, President of the City Fire Fighters Association. "Both men," said Tate, "have shown that they do know what has been going on at the Philadelphia General Hospital, and that they can be of some help in its operation."[13] Subsequently, a special ward was set up for the treatment of policemen and firemen only.

New York City

When Mayor Lindsay invited Howard Leary to leave his post in Philadelphia and become Police Commissioner in New York City—the first ever to come from out of state—he was most impressed with Leary's record of careful treatment of dissident groups and his interest in establishing good police relations with ghetto residents. Table 5-1 shows that Mr. Leary did indeed assume leadership in this highly sensitive area, more so than any of the other key New York participants.

The Commissioner's leading strategy was to devise new programs which would help to recruit more minority group persons into the Police Department. Civil rights leaders had long complained that too few of the City's policemen were black or Puerto Rican. Though the Police Department had always been reluctant to reveal hard data on this question, a study group created by President Kennedy in 1963 (the Lawyer's Committee for Civil Rights Under Law) confirmed this allegation. It showed that New York City had a smaller percentage of black policemen than three other major cities in the country: While only 5 percent of New York's policemen were black (1,355 out of a total of 27,112 policemen), Baltimore's police force was about one-third black, Chicago's police force was about one-quarter black and Philadelphia's department was about one-fifth black.

Soon after taking command, Leary and the Lindsay staff instituted a drive to recruit one thousand disadvantaged youths for a new police cadet corps. Financed by a 2.9 billion dollar federal grant, the program was intended as a cram course to prepare black and Puerto Rican youths for the Police Department's competitive entrance tests. Of the initial group of cadets, eight hundred were drop-outs from school. Anticipating criticism from the policemen's organizations, Commissioner Leary and Mayor Lindsay made it clear that the program would "absolutely not" reduce the quality of the police force since the examinations for patrolmen's jobs were unchanged.

A few months later in the Summer of 1966, Leary opened another campaign to recruit blacks and Puerto Ricans directly into the Police Department. Police recruiting teams, usually including a member of each of the aforementioned minorities, were sent out to local beaches, baseball games, jazz concerts and movie theaters to distribute literature and recruitment applications. In phase two of this program, police officials traveled to such places as Boston, Philadelphia, Baltimore, Washington, D.C., and Atlanta to entice college and high school students.

Efforts to bring minority persons into the Police Department did not impress the leadership of the Patrolmen's Benevolent Association. Reflecting the feelings of his following, P.B.A. President John J. Cassese criticized the cadet corps program as being unfair to youths who were not black or Puerto Rican.[14] A more strategic opportunity to express opposition came along in May of 1967 when the New York City Civil Service Commission proposed revoking a regulation that automatically barred persons convicted of petit larceny from becoming eligible for jobs as policemen or firemen. The proposal was an attempt by the Commission to increase the number of such jobs available to members of minority groups, many of whom grew up in ghettos where it was easy to get into trouble with the law. As one official explained, the proposed change would help persons who had been "unfairly" convicted in their youth.

But Norman Frank, the P.B.A.'s community relations counsel let it be known that his organization would "vigorously oppose that change or any other dilution of the entrance requirements for police service. . . . We are trying constantly to upgrade the quality and qualifications of those who pursue a law-enforcement career. This objective will be totally destroyed if the present amendment by the Civil Service Commission is adopted."[15] Gerald J. Ryan, President of the Uniformed Firemen's Association concurred: "Firefighters are professional men, and, as such, the requirements for admittance into the Fire Department must continue to be based on the most stringent qualifications as to physical and mental ability and character."[16] Such testimony was enough to squelch the idea. In concluding their deliberations that had begun a year earlier, the three-man commission quietly tabled the proposal.

In the meanwhile other strategies were being pursued. Complementing his concern over minority group recruitment, Commissioner Leary also sought to improve police communication with ghetto residents. In February of

1967 he helped establish a committee called PACT, Police and Citizens Together, to encourage closer ties between the police and the community. Although the Police Department had a number of grass roots programs to ease tensions in the ghetto areas, it had no such organization at the headquarters level. Leary explained that the Committee would "work . . . at a very high level providing the necessary guidance and counsel to develop programs."[17] Accordingly, one such program which was instituted by the Police Department in October of 1969 was called Prevention Enforcement Patrol (PEP). This consisted of a special squad of young black and Puerto Rican policemen who were raised in the slums who would work in Harlem on a volunteer basis. Commandered by a black officer, the underlying rationale was that this group knew the streets and the people and would show special sensitivity to community problems.

In contrast to the role of the Police Commissioner, the findings in Table 5-1 show that Mayor Lindsay's activities in the area of police-community relations were limited. Where the Mayor did assert himself, it was to assure improved coordination of the police with other public and civic bodies. For example, in March of 1967 he established the Criminal Justice Coordinating Council which was given the responsibility of unifying the efforts of the police, the courts, the district attorneys, corrections and other crime related bodies. Members of civic, labor, professional and business groups were also appointed to the Council to represent community interests.

As referred to previously, Mayor Lindsay also appointed a special group in March of 1968 to assure proper arrest and judicial procedures during civil disturbances. Known as the Committee on Administration of Criminal Justice Under Emergency Conditions, it consisted of the Police Commissioner, the five county district attorneys and a representation of the bar associations in New York City. Working alongside this group would be a parallel Courts Committee on Civil Disorders. Deputy Mayor Robert W. Sweet and Corporation Counsel J. Lee Rankin, it was announced, would provide direction as cochairmen.

By-and-large the Mayor and his Commissioner managed to avoid excessive controversy in this sensitive area. One ticklish issue that could not be avoided, however, pertained to the question of police membership in the John Birch Society. At the time he was first sworn into office, Commissioner Leary was asked by newsmen if he planned to permit policemen to belong to the John Birch Society. The issue of policemen's membership in the society had spurred controversy in Philadelphia and other cities across the country. Critics argued that this militantly anti-Communist group was anti-Semitic and that it had been hostile to civil rights activity.

Leary's reply was that he would follow the same practice as the Philadelphia Police Department which he had directed for three years. This was to let Birch Society members stay on the force if they gave assurances that their membership would in no way affect their police judgment. Leary continued: "If those persons desirous of membership in the John Birch Society are not taking a position contrary to the policies and practices of the New York City Police Department" or to the Federal or State Constitution and the City Charter, "we find no fault with that."[18]

Lindsay, however, was not so sure that this was the correct response and declared that the organization was "hostile to everything decent." Department rules stated that no member of the force may belong to a political club or take active part in the nomination or election of candidates for public office. In March of 1966, two joint legislative committees of the State of New York held hearings on the question and concluded that the John Birch Society was a political organization. The committees report, which was advisory only, said that despite protests by the organization that it was purely an educational group, its official documents proved its political nature. Thus, any policeman who belonged to it violated the State Penal Law.

At the committee hearings, Commissioner Leary called the Birch Society "abhorrent" and said he would forbid policemen to belong "if I had the authority." He added he would consult with Corporation Counsel J. Lee Rankin "and be guided by his opinion" as to whether policemen could legally be members of the society. In May of 1966, over the outcries of such groups as the Anti-Defamation League of B'nai Brith and the National Association for the Advancement of Colored People, the Lindsay administration's chief counsel ruled that the Birch Society did not fall into the legal definition of a political organization and it was therefore legal for policemen to belong to it.

By using his political acumen, Leary managed to save himself from what could have been a severe blow—the alienation of minority groups and members of the liberal establishment whose support he needed in carrying out his programs. By tossing the issue into the Corporation Counsel's lap, Mr. Leary was able to displace much of the criticism at the same time that he turned a political question into a legal one.

It can be suggested, also, that Mayor Lindsay sought to avoid just such a pitfall by deliberately adopting a distant role on questions of police-community relations. As a self-proclaimed reform Mayor who relied on black, Hispanic and liberal support, it was generally expected that he would assert greater leadership on such matters. Lindsay appears to have preferred caution, however. As a means of keeping tabs on community trouble spots and easing tensions, the

Mayor seemed to rely most heavily on the Urban Task Force, a civil agency which was headed by Barry Gottehrer, one of his own assistants. On one occasion where he did step out to oppose a P.B.A. proposal which would allow policemen to hold outside jobs up to twenty hours a week, but he was overruled by the state legislature.

Chicago

In Chicago, the police establishment as well as the Mayor appear to be uninterested in police–community relations. As revealed in Table 5-1, there is little evidence of action whether it be successes or defeats. For the most part, the initiative on such matters comes from others not formerly a part of the public arena. A careful viewing of successes, furthermore, shows as much effort directed toward the vetoing of proposals as toward the initiating of proposals.

In the face of growing acrimony between the police and black ghetto residents during the period 1966 to 1969, it is indicative that only two new programs were instituted to allay tensions. One of the programs was established in the Summer of 1966 by the Robert R. McCormick Charitable Trust (deeded by the will of Colonel Robert R. McCormick, late publisher of the Chicago Tribune). It contributed a major portion of the funding needed to educate select city policemen in the Spanish language and culture. Initially about one hundred fifty policemen from mostly Puerto Rican districts took the courses two hours a day, four days a week for two months at Chicago City Junior College. The other program was authorized by Superintendent O.W. Wilson in March of 1967 when he appointed "District Community Service Sergeants" in eighteen police districts. These sergeants were assigned to assist the District Commanders in furthering community relations, to maintain contact with neighborhood groups and to keep the district commander informed of problems.

The District Community Service Sergeants program, we should note, grew out of discussions between O.W. Wilson and Thomas R. Mulroy, the Chairman of Mayor Richard Daley's Citizens' Committee to Study Police–Community Relations. This Committee was established in the Spring of 1966 by the Mayor in response to growing complaints by black ghetto residents of police brutality. Its final report titled "Police and Public," (published in May of 1967) is interesting for what it reveals of the city's official attitude toward the police role.[19] Much of the report is devoted to discussions of the inadequacies of various review procedures which had been instituted in other places such as a civilian police review board or an ombudsman which could evaluate citizen complaints against police officers. The report did recommend continuation or enlargement of existing Chicago programs such as "Officer Friendly" school visitations and a Police Community Workshop program. The Sergeants program represented the only really new proposal to be recommended by the Committee.

Other community issues which crystallized during the period 1966 to 1969 were more controversial in tone. In December of 1967, a police internal security unit found that a Ku Klux Klan cell, equipped with guns, ammunition and hand grenades, existed within the Chicago Police Department. (The telltale clue were the letters K.K.K. painted in white on the trunk of an automobile that one of the Klan members was driving to and from his beat.) Taken aback by the revelation, Police Superintendent Conlisk told a press conference that he was shocked by evidence which linked at least six patrolmen to this "hate" organization. Moving to dismiss the officers on the grounds that they violated the rules of the Police Department, he explained that "this department intends to maintain its image and integrity and will actively investigate any policeman associated with hate groups."[20]

In the eyes of Conlisk and other ranking police officers, extremism of any form was to be excoriated. This included not only groups like the K.K.K., but "antisocial" street gangs as well. Thus another source of consternation to the police was the Woodlawn Organization, a black community action group on Chicago's South Side which had received a federal grant to work with black gangs. The grant came under fire from city authorities because it went directly to the Woodlawn organization bypassing City Hall. This alone, among all poverty projects, was outside the Mayor's domain.

In the Spring of 1968 when refunding from the Office of Economic Opportunity seemed imminent, the elite gang intelligence unit of the Chicago police force moved into action. Derogatory information was volunteered to the United States Senate's special subcommittee on investigations headed by John L. McClellan of Arkansas. The subcommittee had been investigating urban rioting and was concerned over the role played by two Chicago gangs, the Blackstone Rangers and the Disciples, during the riots that followed the assassination of the Reverend Martin Luther King. This was in spite of reports that the Blackstone Rangers kept their Woodlawn area quiet during the time that other black neighborhoods in the city were being burned and looted.

Testimony from the police and other witnesses during the hearings was highly incriminating. Among those singled out for complicity was the Reverend John Fry. Police officers testified that the Blackstone Rangers were considered a "street gang with no status whatsoever" until Reverend Fry began serving the group as a counselor. It was alleged that the gang was holding clandestine meetings in Fry's First Presbyterian church, buying arms, threatening and intimidating members, trafficking in drugs and planning crime and violence in the neighborhood.

In light of the bad publicity, the OEO had little choice but to deny renewal of the Woodlawn grant. As acting director of the OEO pending Senate confirmation, Bertrand Hardy was vulnerable to pressure. In reply to a letter of inquiry from Senator Harry Byrd of Virginia, Hardy gave assurance that it was not OEO's intention to "subsidize gangs of hoodlums in Chicago. . . ." "I have no intention of approving the type of project in Chicago or elsewhere . . . which would produce the objectionable results of this particular grant."[21]

With the terminations of the Woodlawn project, the police gang intelligence unit was able to resume full command within its special jurisdiction. But not all citizens were convinced that this represented any kind of solution to the gang problem. As an open pronouncement of such feelings, black Alderman A.A. Rayner, Jr. submitted an amendment to the City Council in December of 1969 which proposed ending the police gang unit. In an accompanying resolution he termed the unit repressive and contended it had damaged Chicago and failed to reduce crime. Alderman Leon Despres, whose ward included many blacks agreed. "Studies show that any attempt to repress gangs has the opposite effect," he said. "You should deal with crimes, but not repress the gangs themselves. To break up and shoot simply solidifies the gangs."[22] By a forty to three vote, the Council rejected the proposal.

NOTES

1. See, for example, *Report of the National Advisory Commission on Civil Disorders, op. cit.*, chap. 11; *Task Force Report: The Police. op. cit.*, chap. 6.
2. Joseph D. Lohman and Gordon E. Misner, *The Police and the Community*, A Report Prepared for The President's Commission on Law Enforcement and Administration of Justice, Vol. 2, (Washington, D.C.: U.S. Government Printing Office, October, 1966), p. 62.
3. *Ibid.*, p. 62.
4. *The Philadelphia Inquirer*, November 26, 1967.
5. *Ibid.*, May 30, 1969.
6. *Ibid.*, June 4, 1969.
7. *Ibid.*, June 10, 1969.
8. *Ibid.*
9. *Ibid.*, June 30, 1969.
10. *Ibid.*
11. *Ibid.*
12. *Ibid.*, July 11, 1969.
13. *Ibid.*, January 23, 1968.
14. *The New York Times*, March 29, 1966.
15. *Ibid.*, May 15, 1967.
16. *Ibid.*

17. *Ibid.,* February 6, 1967.
18. *Ibid.,* February 22, 1967.
19. This report was widely distributed throughout the country. See *Police and Public: A Critique and a Program,* Final Report of the Citizens' Committee to Study Police–Community Relations in the City of Chicago to Mayor Richard J. Daley (May 22, 1967).
20. *Chicago Tribune,* December 29, 1967.
21. *Ibid.,* September 4, 1968.
22. *Ibid.,* December 31, 1969.

Chapter Six

Models of Police Politics

AN OVERVIEW

Table 6-1 gives us an overall view of the successes and defeats of key participants in the making of police policy. As a first observation, we can note the many defeats experienced by all the New York City participants—a pattern not evident in the other two cities. While the Patrolmen's Benevolent Association appears to lead in defeats (the Law Enforcement Group is responsible for one of the nine defeats listed for policemen's associations), it would be a mistake to overlook the fact that it has also scored about as many victories as Philadelphia's Fraternal Order of the Police. In Chicago, the policemen's organizations (a total of three major ones claim to represent patrolmen's professional interests) appear to have no visible influence, while it is the Mayor who looms forth as a man of unchallenged authority.

In viewing police commissioners, the ones in New York and Philadelphia appear to have asserted strong leadership. But the fact that New York's Commissioner shows six defeats as compared to only two in Philadelphia would seem to indicate a greater degree of countervailing power in the former city. The same can be said in assessing the mayoralty roles in these two cities.

To probe further, it would be useful to consider the special kinds of relationships which exist among the key participants. To what extent have these persons and groups been mutually supportive or mutually antagonistic? The findings in Table 6–2 provide us with some clues to conflict relations. In looking at New York City, we see that a favorite target of both the Mayor and the Commissioner has been the policemen's association (P.B.A.); and, as to be expected, the policemen's association has managed to inflict the most setbacks on the Mayor and the Commissioner. The totals for New York City indicate that here indeed is the source of most of the conflict. Philadelphia, on the other

79

Table 6-1.   Total Successes and Defeats of Key Participants

	New York City		Philadelphia		Chicago	
	Successes	Defeats	Successes	Defeats	Successes	Defeats
Mayor	11	5	12	1	21	—
Cmnr./Supt.	14	6	11	2	5	2
Police officers/Dept.	1	3	5	1	3	7
Policemen's assns.	7	9	6	1	—	—

Note: Totals in this table are a little less than the equivalent of total figures in the previous tables since data was sometimes included twice when found to be applicable to more than one category, e.g., police accountability and law and order.

Table 6-2.   Conflict Relations in All Three Issue Areas According to Contributors and Subjects of Defeat

	Subjects of defeat														
	Mayor			Cmnr./Supt.			Police officers/Dept.			Policemen's assns.			Total*		
Contributors to defeat	NYC	Phil.	C	NYC	Phil.	C	NYC	Phil.	C	NYC	Phil.	C	NYC	Phil.	C
Mayor	—	—	—	2	1	1	—	—	—	4	—	—	6	1	1
Cmnr./Supt.	—	—	—	—	—	—	—	—	—	5	—	—	5	—	—
Police officers/Dept.	—	—	—	—	—	—	—	—	—	—	—	—	—	—	—
Policemen's assns.	5	—	—	2	—	1	3	—	7	—	—	—	10	—	8
Others	—	1	—	—	—	—	—	1	—	5	2	—	5	4	—
													26	5	9

*Total conflict relations amounts to more than total defeats as more than one person or agency can oppose a particular decision.

hand, shows only five defeats in all, and four of these originated from other sources. Among the key actors—Mayor, Commission, FOP, ranking police officers— there is virtually no visible conflict. Chicago presents a similar picture. Almost all contributors of defeats are from outside the mayor-police orbit and, we might add, from outside the city.

Not to be overlooked, however, are some important differences between Philadelphia and Chicago. In the latter place, as we saw in Table 6-1, it is the Mayor who exercises unchallenged leadership. No one person or group in the police establishment competes or even comes close to competing with him. In Philadelphia, the Mayor shares power with the Police Commissioner; and since 1967 when Rizzo assumed office, the Commissioner had actually shown greater leadership. The F.O.P. and ranking police officers must also be counted among the influential. As a coalition of interests they have all contributed to the making of police policy. But just as important, as noted in Table 5-1, is the ability of this coalition to establish itself in other community jurisdictions which are only indirectly related to police affairs.

POWER RESOURCES AND STRATEGIES

If the police have come to intervene actively in the political affairs of com- munities, it is necessary to inquire into how this has been brought about. What remains to be explored are the special kinds of political resources and strategies which are available to the police and which typify police politics in each of our three sample cities.

New York City

As the Democratic party organization in New York City began to decline during the late 1950's and early 1960's—the last of the old Tammany leaders, Carmine DeSapio, lost his office in 1961—city politics became a free- wheeling, multifactioned affair. During this time, the Patrolmen's Benevolent Association entered the political lists just as other groups and organizations were inclined to do.

An unintentional contributor to the politicization of the New York police was Stephen P. Kennedy who served as Police Commissioner from 1955 to 1961. Though he was a career man who had worked his way up through the ranks, Kennedy was seen by his men as a reform type. To the bane of his patrol- men, Kennedy stressed formal education as a condition for promotion and carried out widespread transfers along with a "shoofly" [1] system to combat corruption and achieve "efficiency." When it was once suggested that he ought to be a little more diplomatic in his relations with others, he replied, "A police commissioner must not only meet the practical problems from day to day, he must be a strong moral force. He must not bow to expediency or to political considerations."[2]

In August of 1960, an investigation had revealed that some policemen were "moonlighting" on other jobs to supplement their incomes. Citing police regulations which forbade this, Kennedy dismissed three policemen and imposed disciplinary penalties on thirteen others. This action quickly led to a bitter struggle between the Commissioner and his men.

President John Cassese of the P.B.A. complained that the penalties imposed on the policemen were too harsh and attacked the moonlighting rule. He stated that policemen who worked on second jobs deserved praise for their initiative and he estimated that sixty to seventy percent of the police force were moonlighting because of inadequate pay. But the Commissioner was unyielding on this issue and when he fined the thirteen men involved in moonlighting and placed them on probation for a year, P.B.A. delegates voted to pay the policemen their salaries through a special solicitation. Kennedy countered this decision by prohibiting the solicitation of any funds and by warning that he would bring departmental charges against anyone who did. On the same day that this pronouncement was made, ten more policemen were fined for moonlighting.

There is no clear evidence as to how it started, but in October of 1960, policemen began to effect a slowdown. Cassese disclaimed any responsibility and insisted that the idea of ticketing only major violations originated in the precincts. When the slowdown seemed to have some effect, the Commissioner was enraged. He termed the action a "strike" and considered it "treason to the people." Referring to the P.B.A., Kennedy exclaimed:

> As long as I am Police Commissioner, political pressure groups are not going to dictate policy. No freewheeling, self–dealing bureaucracy answerable to no one but themselves is going to subvert the discipline of the Police Department by strikes or other derelictions of sworn duty whether inspired or planned by the present leadership of the P.B.A. or any other irresponsible group. Apparently some never learned the lessons of the Boston police strike. What was valid then is valid now.[3]

Nor was Kennedy above retribution. Upon discovering that Cassese's automobile was usually parked between "No Parking" signs near P.B.A. headquarters, the Commissioner considered this dereliction justification for transferring the P.B.A. official out of his desk job to street duty. Cassese described his transfer as "another example of personal vengeance for fighting in behalf of members of the department." [4]

At this point, patrolmen adopted a new tactic. Instead of carrying forth with their slowdown, they began to issue large numbers of tickets. As this continued over several weeks, the newspapers printed box scores of ticket distributions. But Kennedy could not be moved by this strategy and after four weeks, he proudly announced that traffic deaths declined by 43 percent and injuries by 14 percent over the year before.

Striving to regain the initiative, the P.B.A. charged in newspaper advertisements that Kennedy had established traffic ticket quotas and had given out prizes for the policemen who gave the most tickets. To publicize their grievances, five hundred P.B.A. wives picketed City Hall protesting the moonlighting rules. In their attempt to build up additional pressure, P.B.A. delegates called a meeting to consider the possibility of ousting Kennedy who was a full-fledged member of the Association. They also amended the by-laws to permit Cassese to continue as President of the P.B.A. if he felt compelled to retire from the police force.

The day after the meeting, Kennedy appeared on television and publicly showed his defiance by ripping up his P.B.A. membership card. After taping the card together again, he repeated the performance before reporters and photographers who missed the earlier version. The P.B.A. countered by ousting the Commissioner officially. Consequently, to justify his behavior, Commissioner Kennedy tried to explain what he considered to be the fundamental issue: "This isn't a fight over moonlighting or ticket quotas. This is a power play. What they are after is controlling policy. And they're not going to get it. Not while I'm the Commissioner." [5]

In January 1961, the New York State Supreme Court upheld the Commissioner's right to bar moonlighting. Kennedy declared himself vindicated and a few months later he resigned from office. But if the P.B.A. lost the battle, members were prepared to argue that they had won the war. One observor, James Priest Gifford, contends that "even if it was not true that Cassese had forced Kennedy out, it was important that many policemen interpreted the situation that way." [6] Gifford continues:

> Certainly once the echoes of the name-calling had ceased, the P.B.A. found itself a much more united group than it had been for perhaps as long as two decades, and Stephen P. Kennedy deserved much of the credit for that new-found unity. A group which had been frequently apathetic at its best and bitterly split at its worst now

was aroused and together in defending itself against what many regarded as a mortal threat.[7]

By "taking-on" the Commissioner, John Cassese became a hero to the P.B.A. membership thereby consolidating his leadership early in his tenure as President. More importantly, the experience of the moonlighting contest provided opportunity for a testing of political tactics which could be used and built upon in later battles. The civilian review board controversy provided just that opportunity.

In the Summer of 1965 when several civilian review bills were being considered by the City Council, the P.B.A. rallied five thousand off-duty policemen to picket City Hall—"the largest police turnout ever," according to one observor.[8] This demonstration was followed up with a drive that collected five hundred thousand signatures on a petition protesting a civilian review plan that the Council was seriously weighing. Soon after, the P.B.A. introduced a bill in the New York State Legislature for the purpose of blocking civilian review; it did not pass. Then, in the Spring of 1966, the P.B.A. went to court seeking to prevent the creation of a review board.

When that effort also failed, the Association initiated a campaign for a referendum to change the City Charter. During the summer, "friends and relatives" gathered close to fifty-two thousand signatures for the purpose of placing the issue on the ballot. Some forty thousand signatures were collected in a similar effort by the Conservative Party. It was proposed that the City Charter be amended so as to bar civilians from boards reviewing police actions.

With racial tensions running high, the New York Civil Liberties Union accused President Cassese of "injecting a thinly veiled racism" in his attacks on the board. As we noted in a previous chapter, the City challenged the legality of the referendum, but the courts held that the question had a place on the ballot. Thus, the stage was set for a referendum campaign which became one of the most bitterly fought political contests in the history of the city.

Support for the review board came from civil liberties, labor, and liberal groups who banded together under the banner of the Federated Associations for Impartial Review (FAIR). Constituent organizations included the American Jewish Committee, the B'nai Brith Anti-Defamation League, the Liberal Party, the Citizen Union, the Guardians Association (the organization of black policemen) and several lawyers groups. The dominant organization was the New York Civil Liberties Union. New York Senators Jacob Javits and Robert F. Kennedy, gubernatorial candidates Frank O'Connor and Franklin D. Roosevelt Jr., former U.S. Attorney General Herbert Brownell and other prominent citizens also committed themselves against the PBA-sponsored referendum.

Opponents of civil review included the Conservative Party, various American Legion posts, parents and taxpayers groups who had been opposed to school-busing, homeowners groups and the Brooklyn Bar Association. These were organized into the Independent Citizens Committee Against Review Boards, with the P.B.A. as the dominant group. The P.B.A. went on record as "being prepared to spend its whole treasury" of $1.5-million to fight civilian review.[9]

The tone of the campaign was revealed in the Committee's first advertisement. It showed a young attractive white girl in a white coat coming out of a subway entrance onto a dark street. Across the bottom of the picture is the warning: "The Civilian Review Board must be stopped! Her life . . . your life . . . may depend on it. Send your contribution today!" The text of the advertisement elaborated on the theme. "A police officer must not hesitate. If he does, because he fears the possibility of unjust censure, or, if he feels his job, pension or reputation is threatened, the security and safety of your family may be jeopardized."[10] Other newspaper ads and television commercials continued to play on this theme.

Police Commissioner Leary viewed such advertising as a scare tactic. "The suggestion has been made . . . that the existence of a civilian complaint review board reduces the effectiveness of the police and thereby threatens the safety of the people of New York. This suggestion is totally without foundation."[11] But Leary and other proponents of police review had difficulty in getting their message across to the public. The FAIR campaign suffered from the fact that it depended almost entirely on volunteers. Its basic strategy, moreover, was directed at preventing the referendum from getting on the ballot. This was not finally decided until September which meant that FAIR's strategists had little time in which to fight the ongoing efforts of the P.B.A. and the Independent Citizens Committee. Emphasizing "safety in the streets," the Committee used some twenty-five thousand workers to reach as many voters as possible.

At the final count, it was clear that proponents of civilian review never had a chance. New Yorkers voted overwhelmingly to abolish the Police Department's Civilian Complaint Review Board: 1,313,161 to 765,468. According to David Garth, the campaign manager of FAIR, the real message conveyed during the campaign was fear and his group did not have enough funds to counteract the effects of this. "When you have TV commercials going for four weeks, you're going to make your point. Money was a tremendous problem for us. Our campaign spent $100,000. The real big money did not come to us. You don't win campaigns without money for TV commercials."[12] It was estimated that forces opposing the board spend between $500,000 to $1-million in the campaign.

A post-election survey conducted among a random sample of voters came up with the following findings:

> The CRB referendum proved to be a rout for civil rights forces. For the first time in years, New York City's electorate rejected a liberal position on the ballot. The referendum appeared to intensify basic intergroup cleavages. . . . Blacks voted overwhelmingly for the board. Irish and Italian Catholics, apparently because of their group identification with the police force and their large representation in the working and lower–middle classes, opposed the board by a huge majority. Jews were divided roughly according to their attitudes toward the direction of the civil rights movement.[13]

What was happening, then, was that public opinion in New York City was shifting to the right on the issue of law and order and the police were able to benefit from this in the referendum context. And as evidenced in the 1969 mayoralty campaign, the police would try to capitalize on this new-found constituency. Most significant is the fact that persons with law enforcement background were now prepared to play an openly activist role in city elections.

In the Spring of 1969, Mayor John Lindsay selected Sanford D. Garelik, Chief Inspector of the Police Department as his running-mate for City Council President. Lindsay's strategy was obvious. His campaign advisers were predicting that with Garelik on the ticket, Democrats and conservative Republicans running for Mayor would have a difficult time making rising crime an anti-Lindsay issue. Lindsay's reasons for this choice were presented at a news conference.

> The issue of crime and safety has become a dominant concern in every major city in the country. It demands, in the least, legislative leadership that knows the problem, that can offer more than slogans or bombast, that has had the personal experience to design effective tools for improving the public safety.[14]

When it was his turn to make a statement, Garelik echoed the same theme.

> I do not seek office as a politician—I am not a politician. . . . We do not have adequate public safety. We have come far, and have done much; we must go farther and do much more. The safety of the individual must be guaranteed.[15]

It wasn't long before P.B.A. officials started getting into the act. One such person was Norman Frank, the public-relations, investment and collective bargaining consultant to the P.B.A. and close collaborator to John J. Cassese. Frank briefly announced himself as a mayoral candidate only to withdraw for the purpose of serving as finance chairman for Controller Mario A. Procaccino's mayoralty campaign. Procaccino was recognized as a "law and order" candidate in the Democratic party. When dissident P.B.A. members accused Frank of using union welfare funds for the benefit of a company in which he had vested interests, he was forced to forgo his role in the Procaccino camp.

Ten days later on June 18, John J. Cassese announced his resignation as President of the P.B.A. in order to devote his "full efforts" to the campaign of Procaccino. This happened less than twelve hours after it became known that New York voters had selected Mr. Procaccino in the primary to head the Democratic ticket. Cassese denied that his resignation was in anyway related to the charges that had been made against Norman Frank. Calling crime and fear the central challenge facing New York, Cassese explained that "the results of yesterday's election have given me hope that we may soon have an administration which will devote itself, at long last, to solving that fundamental problem—not only by permitting more effective law enforcement, but by effecting genuine social progress."[16] Asked whether Procaccino had offered him any position in city government—such as Police Commissioner—if he won, Cassese replied: "That's for the future."[17]

Another political hopeful was former Police Commissioner Vincent L. Broderick who had announced his candidacy for the Democratic nomination for Controller. Like the others, he too was preoccupied with the issue of crime in the streets. But in addition, as he explained in a news conference, the question of "political interference" with the police was foremost in his mind. He asserted that one reason Lindsay did not reappoint him as Commissioner in 1966 was because the Mayor knew he would not tolerate political interference with the Police Department.

Of all the law-enforcement candidates to formally enter the 1969 election battle, only Sanford Garelik made it all the way on a Republican–Liberal Independent ticket. He received 1,074,436 votes, 92,618 more than his running mate, Mayor Lindsay. Though also victorious in his race for mayor, it was clear that Lindsay had no popular mandate. With the opposition divided among two "law and order" opponents, he won with only 42 percent of the total vote.

Philadelphia

As in New York City, the traditional party organizations of Philadelphia have also been subject to deterioration—first, the Republican machine which had been dominant until the early 1950's and most recently, the Democratic party. The end-results of this condition were illustrated in the 1967 election when the incumbent Democratic Mayor James J. Tate was denied his party's endorsement in light of preelection polls which were predicting his defeat.

It is at this time that an important series of events took place—events which were to drastically change the political style of the city. In a meeting of the City Democratic Committee on March 11, 1967, a majority of Democratic ward leaders slated former City Controller Alexander Hemphill as its candidate for Mayor. Tate's fifteen minute speech pleading for support could not sway them. That same evening, the police began a crackdown in Philadelphia taprooms on alleged liquor law violations. The raids continued through the weekend during which time the police entered over one hundred bars and arrested over three hundred persons.

Though the Mayor denied it, tavern owners were insisting that Tate ordered the raids as a warning to his democratic opponents. *The Philadelphia Inquirer* quoted one police lieutenant as saying that he and his men were "disgusted" at what they considered "politically inspired" revenge against some ward leaders.[18] When the Tavern Owners Association attempted to send a committee to Tate and Police Commissioner Edward J. Bell to demand an explanation for the crackdown, it was reported back that the two were unavailable.

A month later Police Commissioner Bell, suffering from hypertension, took a leave of absence; and Deputy Commissioner Frank Rizzo was put in full command of the Police Department. City Administrator Frank Corleto disclosed that Rizzo was Mayor Tate's personal choice for the job. On May 16, the very same day on which Tate won the primary election, Police Commissioner Bell resigned from the post he had held for only fifteen months. Mayor Tate announced that Frank Rizzo would take over the job immediately. Although Bell cited health as his reason for leaving, the real cause according to news accounts was "his sore disillusionment with the cynicism of Philadelphia politics and demands made upon him by Tate that he involve the police in political affairs."[19] The press report continues as follows:

> According to a number of reliable sources, Tate and Bell had their first serious falling out in March at one of the Mayor's regular weekly meetings of his department commissioners. In essence, Tate told the commissioners that he was in a fight for his life with the Democratic city organization; that it was not "my fight alone"; that every ranking official in City Hall would be unseated if he lost the mayoralty election.
>
> This speech was a tacit demand that the city departments mobilize behind Tate. Bell resisted. He told Tate he did not think the police should become involved in politics. Tate called this attitude "disloyalty." And Bell soon learned the price.[20]

If, indeed, the police were engaged in politics as reported, this was not the first time. The key question, however, is politics under whose auspices. The politicization of the Philadelphia police had been building even during the reform administration of Mayor J. Richardson Dilworth when the city became the first in the nation to establish a civilian review board. While the City Council was considering such a board in early 1958, the President of the local Fraternal Order of Police threatened that there would be "a revolt in the department if this new board idea goes through."[21] It was the civilian review board issue that contributed directly to a new awareness of the political potential of the police bureaucracy acting in its own behalf.

About a year after the Police Review Board had been in operation, the F.O.P. brought suit in behalf of seven men awaiting hearings before the Board. The F.O.P. argument was that the Board disciplined police personnel in violation of the City Charter. The Charter specified that civilian boards created to oversee city agencies were to be advisory, with each agency retaining disciplinary authority over its personnel. Philadelphia Common Pleas Court decided for the F.O.P. position.

Before the city could appeal the decision, the F.O.P. leadership and Board members announced a compromise. The agreements reached were as follows: (1) The name "Police Review Board" would be changed to "Police Advisory Board." (2) The Board's rule would be modified so as to provide that the Board may "request" instead of "order" a police investigation. (3) The Board would send its report to the Mayor instead of the Police Commissioner. (4) Members of the Police Department whose attendance was desired by the Board would receive notice from the Police Commissioner instead of from the Board directly. (5) The Board would not hold a hearing in connection with a complaint against a member of the police force while related criminal proceedings were pending against that member unless he requested that the hearing be held. (6) The fact that criminal proceedings were pending against the complainant, however, would not cause a postponement of Board hearings. (7) An exact copy of the complaint filed with the Board would be transmitted to the policeman or his counsel.

From February 1960, when the settlement was achieved, until the Summer of 1964, the Advisory Board issue remained in the background of Philadelphia politics. This changed rather abruptly, however, when John Harrington, a sergeant in the elite Highway Patrol unit, led an insurgent slate to victory in the local F.O.P. elections. Playing on the theme that respect for law-enforcement was diminishing, Harrington had been an unsuccessful candidate for the F.O.P. presidency in 1960 and 1962. Upon being elected, Harrington did not mince words in conveying his view of how the F.O.P. would relate to

Philadelphia's political leaders: "We owe nothing to the guys in the big stone house (Philadelphia's City Hall) and we don't have to walk around there in sneakers."[22]

Following up on this declaration, Harrington initiated a new campaign against the Police Advisory Board. When a delegation of New York City Councilmen visited Philadelphia in July to get a first hand view of how such an agency would work in New York City, Harrington testified that it lowered police morale and efficiency. A few weeks later he stated that the Board's prime function was "to pacify the people who live in the low class areas with police records."[23]

The Harrington–F.O.P. leadership asserted that the city riots of 1964 lasted as long as they did only because Philadelphia policemen were fearful of using adequate force less they be brought before the P.A.B. Harrington elaborated as follows:

> You saw the pictures of the cannibals coming out of the stores with t.v. sets on their heads. If it hadn't been for the P.A.B. we would have grabbed them and if they resisted hit them with our black jacks.[24]

Harrington's unrelenting battle against the Philadelphia Board bore implications which carried beyond the city itself. During a time when Rochester had established a civilian review board and New York City was considering legislation to create one, Harrington was able to use his Philadelphia experience to capture the presidency of the national F.O.P. in 1965.

A short time after winning this national office, Harrington began a series of legal maneuvers against the P.A.B. (The history of court decisions is reviewed in Chapter 3.) Supporting him in this endeavor were the Veterans of Foreign Wars, the Philadelphia Police Chiefs Association, the United Retired Policemen, the Firemen and Park Guards of Philadelphia, and the Federation of Women's Clubs and allied organizations. Standing in opposition to Harrington on the review board issue was the Fellowship Commission, the Philadelphia branch of the American Civil Liberties Union, the Presbyterian–Inter-Racial Council, the Lutheran Church, the Philadelphia Union League, and every civil rights group with the exception of the local N.A.A.C.P. chapter under Cecil Moore. (The N.A.A.C.P. was extremely unhappy over the results of the cases registering citizen complaints. Invariably, action taken by the police officers was supported.)

After Judge Weinrott of the Philadelphia Common Pleas Court ruled that the Police Advisory Board had no authorization in law, Mayor Tate refused to process an appeal. Apparently, the Mayor had changed his mind on the efficacy of civilian review; and two years later, as the Board languished, he abolished it entirely through executive order.

A look at the record of Board decisions during its existence would seem to belie the F.O.P. allegation that the agency harassed the police and lowered law enforcement effectiveness. During the eight years and three months of Board operations, only 1004 complaints were filed. Of this total number of cases, only 207 reached the hearing stage, the others being dismissed or resolved through informal means. Of those 207 cases which went to hearings, the Board recommended an oral or written reprimand in 30 instances and temporary suspension in another 20 cases. Of the total complaints, only 5 percent were terminated with recommendations of punishment. Dismissal was never advised.

In examining the civilian review board struggle in Philadelphia, a more instructive explanation than the pros and cons of law enforcement effectiveness pertains to the political needs of key participants. One such person was John Harrington who ran for the presidency of the F.O.P. local as an insurgent candidate in opposition to the handpicked successor of an outgoing president in 1960, and against an incumbent in 1962 and 1964. Various observors contend that the review board emerged as an issue which was used by Harrington for his own career aspirations. It not only got him the Presidency of the Philadelphia Lodge in 1964, but also the position of national F.O.P. President in 1965. Before Harrington arrived, F.O.P. members had been against the existence of the P.A.B., but never to the degree that Harrington and his followers were prepared to go.

Mayor James Tate also had political needs. If he was to be reelected in 1967, he had to somehow fashion a new coalition of interests to replace his disintegrating party base. Ready–made for the candidate who could effectively exploit the civilian review board issue was the support of numerous "law and order" groups in the city. On the face of it, Tate's decision not to appeal the Weinrott ruling appeared to be based on just that kind of strategy. Another decision which seemed to fit this strategy was the appointment of Frank L. Rizzo to replace ailing Police Commissioner Edward Bell.

Rizzo's reputation as a tough and fearless cop was soon receiving big play in the newspapers. For example, one photo printed during the election campaign showed him rounding up a group of young blacks; another showed him in a crash helmet surrounded by his officers intent on breaking up a black demonstration against a white merchant; a third photo showed him at the head of a flying wedge of policemen breaking into the headquarters of the Revolutionary Action Movement.[25] Tate took an open interest in his new appointee and made an issue of the fact that his Republican opponent, District Attorney Arlen Specter, would not unequivocally agree that Rizzo would stay on if elected. Consequently, when Tate was elected by the very narrow margin of 12,000 votes, Rizzo was given much of the credit.

Most important, according to our findings, is that what James Tate initiated in support of his own cause has since escalated into a new political phenomenon: the coming of age of the police as a power bloc. As a new symbol of electoral potency, Frank Rizzo was given a free hand, and with support from the Fraternal Order of Police, he came to exercise strong influence in a variety of issues. Of special significance has been his leadership on the issue of "law and order." By late 1970, Rizzo's course was set. With the help of Mayor Tate, who was forbidden by the City Charter from seeking a third term, Rizzo was endorsed almost unanimously by the Democratic Committee to run for Mayor. (Only one dissenting vote was recorded.) Shortly thereafter, in the Spring of 1971, Rizzo won a crushing victory in the primary election over the former chairman of the city's Democratic party; and in the fall, he easily won the mayoralty election against Republican Thacher Longstreth.

Chicago

In Chicago, the Cook County Democratic Committee as headed by Mayor Daley is still very much alive—a very different story from either Philadelphia or New York. Theodore Lowi reminds us that "when New York was losing its last machine and entering into the new era of permanent Reform, Chicago's machine politics was just beginning to consolidate."[26] If the police establishment appears impotent here, it's because the machine is too strong. Even Police Superintendent Orlando Wilson, the academic expert who was called in to improve administration, enhanced City Hall control by centralizing procedures and consolidating police districts. Thereafter police collusion with ward leaders and neighborhood interests was more difficult to maintain.

During his tenure, Wilson played what is perhaps the most anomalous role of any of the police commissioners surveyed in this study—a cross between the "professional administrator" who is theoretically immune from politics (i.e., the reform model) and what can be called the "mayor's cop." A number of observers close to the scene contend that Wilson was much less independent than he liked to believe. Called in by Daley to clean up the tarnished image of the Chicago police force, he had to rely on Daley to get things done. This became evident at the very beginning of Wilson's tenure when he attempted to set up an internal investigating unit to seek out police infractions. William Turner reports:

> The powerful Patrolmen's Association called a mass meeting to demand Wilson's ouster, and several thousand officers cheered

lustily as one speaker after another chided "the Professor" and his naive theories. But if the P.B.A. was counting on its customary political support, it was doomed to disappointment. Daley, who had passed the "hands off" signal through the Democratic pipeline, backed his superintendent to the hilt and concurred that the department was justified in "utilizing all investigative procedures and techniques which are legally available to it in ferreting out criminal violations or violations of department regulations by its members." It began to occur to the policemen that the alternative to the IID might well be a civilian review board . . . and the recall movement dwindled away.[27]

Here, then, is an important clue to an understanding of Mayor Daley's control. In contrast to Lindsay of New York City, the Mayor of Chicago has been protective of the police. In spite of the pressure of unending allegations by blacks and civil liberties groups, Daley continues to insist that police review must remain internal through the mechanism of the police Internal Affairs Division (formerly the Internal Inspection Division). When the issue of a civilian review board was raised after the 1966 riots, he avoided it by hand-picking a twenty-three member citizens committee to recommend "ways and means of improving the relationship of the police department with the community."[28] Not unexpectedly, the committee reported back that where they've been created, civilian review boards have not been effective in disciplining police officers. As we noted elsewhere in this book, Daley has been able to engineer similar blue-ribbon vindications of the police almost any time they appear to be in trouble.

At the same time, the Chicago Mayor garners the support of rank and file police officers through his hard-line attitude toward protest groups and demonstrations. As we noted earlier, he bitterly rebuked Superintendent of Police Conlisk for pursuing a policy of restraint during the rioting of April, 1968. On that occasion, Daley publicly ordered the Chicago police to "shoot to kill arsonists" and to "shoot to maim or cripple anyone looting." Again, after the nationally publicized battle at the 1968 Democratic National Convention, Daley went to great lengths to defend his police force while attacking the media and outside agitators.

In such situations, Daley not only makes the key decisions, but what is more important, he has the political muscle of the Democratic party organization to see that his decisions are carried out. Chicago policemen, on the other hand, have not as yet acquired effective organizational resources of their own. Instead of one major policemen's association which sets the tone as is the case in New York City or Philadelphia, there are at least three major groups which are competitive with each other. More often than not, leaders of the Chicago Patrolmen's Association and the Fraternal Order of Police are pitted against the leaders of the Confederation of Police (C.O.P.). So far they have been unable to effect a viable joint council to pool resources and coordinate strategies. Daley and Police Superintendent Conlisk have resisted these organizations as an attempt to dilute their authority—the Police Department has not granted them formal recognition and refuses to engage in collective bargaining.

CONCLUSIONS: THREE MODELS OF POLICE POLITICS

As Southern novelists have romanticized ante bellum plantations, and Western chroniclers have idealized the wild frontier, so have certain "good government" reformers contributed yarns about America's big cities. At the turn of the century, leaders of the Progressive movement set out to change the quality of urban leadership. Attacking the party machine with a vengeance, their special goal was to democratize and rationalize city government. The heart of their program consisted of such innovations as nonpartisan elections, public employment based on "merit," and a host of "nonpolitical" boards and commissions to administer the needs of the community. In addition, efficient, business-like management was viewed as the key to effective public leadership; and though the reformers sought to strengthen the chief executive through broad budgetary and appointive powers, they deplored and tried to strip away his prerogatives of patronage and influence peddling. All this was done in the name of the public interest.

These concerns remain, by and large, the intellectual baggage of urban reform movements in the United States. It is of some irony, however, that the reformers who have been pursuing goals of "good government" have also been unintentionally contributing to something very different. For example, in their desire to free the cities of party control, good government groups have urged the adoption of merit by examination as a necessary criteria for public employment. Civil service, with its built-in guarantees of tenure and promotion, has been viewed as a panacea which would improve the quality of services administered by public personnel. Reformers have failed to understand, however, that power could be effected through the bureaucracy as well as through political parties. Thus in all large cities today, municipal employees, through their associations and unions, are exerting pressure not only for improved salaries and working conditions, but for autonomy of direction as well. Teachers, sanitation workers, clerks and firemen, as well as policemen, strive to defend their "professional status" from the "political interference" of mayors, department heads, and other "politicians." As the number of organized public employees have continued to increase, mayoral control has become ever more tenuous—contingent, for the most part, on the ability to negotiate and bargain rather than to command.

Two other developments must also be considered in accounting for the present plight of many of America's large cities. First, there has been a very substantial influx from the rural South of unskilled blacks into the downtown ghettos of the country's urban centers. The second development pertains to the breakdown of party organizations. In discussing the latter, it is important to note that until the 1940's and 1950's, the party structure (or machine) was an asset likely to provide important support for the mayor's leadership. Most significant has been the use of party to override the worst abuses of governmental fragmentation—a condition typical more or less of most large cities. Councilmen, executive officers, and even judges who functioned within the city could be pressed to "cooperate" by the fear that renomination would be denied or patronage, funds and other favors would be withdrawn. The expansion of the civil service, however, and the growth of public welfare programs seriously weakened the party organization. Without the discipline of party loyalty, the mayor has had to search for other means of influence.

The new structures of influence in our largest cities evade careful definition because of their complexity. For the most part, however, urban observers speak of the prevalence of a tri-partite coalition of interests consisting of the mayor, local businessmen, and the city bureaucracies.[29] (We should recognize that in New York City, the nation's largest city, power relations are more complex than this.) The distribution of influence among these elements necessarily varies from city to city. For example, the business elite of New York City—primarily in banking, investments and advertising—are generally more preoccupied with national and international affairs than with city affairs. But even where the business sector does play a strong community role, as used to be the case in Philadelphia, mayors have come to depend heavily on the professionalized city employees as represented by their spokesmen—union leaders, bureau heads, and commissioners. This pattern has been observed in New York City where, according to Theodore Lowi, a political alliance of Mayor and bureaucrats came into being in the mayoralty election of 1961 [30] At that time incumbent Robert Wagner ran with two other candidates for city-wide office, one of whom had been a career budget official and Director of the Budget Bureau. As we noted in 1969, John V. Lindsay was elected into office after running on the same ticket with a former Chief Inspector of the Police Department; the other part of his ticket consisted of a former City Finance Administrator.

But in New York City, as elsewhere, such alliances are often quite tenuous, lasting only as long as the chief executive can continue to accommodate the bureaucracies. Contrary to the old style party organization which was usually community-wide in scope, the bureaucrats direct their concern to the particular needs of their own agencies. Parties, after all, are dependent on the votes of popular majorities while city employees depend essentially on what can be negotiated in matters of salary, working conditions, and pensions. Where the mayor lacks the ability and resources to meet their demands, or where he appears to threaten their interests, major disruptions can and do occur. Lindsay has experienced this first hand through the entire period that he served in City Hall. We should note that the police were simply one group of public employees among many others that pitched in to do battle with the Mayor.

What has exacerbated this state of affairs to a new and more serious level of concern is the whole question of race and the anxieties which this question generates. Over the past score years, the in-migration and politicization of large numbers of blacks has had a most pervasive impact on big city politics. Usually poor and low-skilled, such persons are rapidly becoming a numerical majority in many of the largest cities in the country (e.g., Washington, D.C., Baltimore, Detroit, and St. Louis). We previously noted that they comprise approximately one-third of the population in Chicago and Philadelphia and about one-fifth of the population in New York City.

As viewed by growing numbers of white citizens, this development is the root cause of a host of key urban problems including school integration, rising welfare rolls, and joblessness. Perhaps most important has been the "law and order" problem, a reflection both of rising crime tolls and rioting on the one hand, and growing white anxiety on the other.[31] Studies by the National Commission on the Causes and Prevention of Violence showed that twenty-six cities with half a million or more residents (about 17 percent of the national population) generate almost 45 percent of all major crimes.[32] Elsewhere the Commission warns that the large cities are on the way to becoming a mixture of "fortresses" and "places of terror," with the wealthy living in privately guarded compounds and residents moving in armored vehicles through "sanitized corridors" linking places of safety.[33] Our three sample cities of New York, Philadelphia and Chicago typify this quite well.

One of the consequences of such developments has been the coming of age of the "law-enforcer" as an active participant in the politics of the city. "Law-enforcers" can be defined as those persons who either manifest law-enforcement skills as part of their background or, lacking this, articulate law-enforcement rhetoric. Philadelphia's Frank Rizzo can be considered the archtype of this new style which has surfaced in such other places as Minneapolis, Detroit, and Los Angeles. We were able to see in this present work that as community tensions rose in Philadelphia, so, too, rose the career possibilities of Police Commissioner Rizzo. When an assault or a shooting took place, Rizzo usually made himself available to the press to remind all good citizens that these are dangerous times and therefore the police must be supported. Indeed, during the late 1960's, Police Department initiative and morale remained high in Philadelphia while the rest of Mayor Tate's administration appeared to be deteriorating. Tate himself was a lame-duck since the City Charter forbad him from running for another term. At the same time, the Democratic organization which he headed had become highly fragmented, and his administration had been rocked by a series of scandals and a general loss of public confidence.

New York City has been subject to similar pressures. This is in spite of the fact that the 1969 mayoralty election was acclaimed by some liberal commentators as one of the nation's "bright-spots." As we saw, "good-government" man John Lindsay, running without support from either major party, won a second term in an uphill battle against two law-and-order candidates. What should not be overlooked, however, is that Lindsay could well have lost if enough white, middle-class voters had concentrated their support on one of his two adversaries. Ignored by election analysts were the motivations for Lindsay's selection of Sanford Garelik, a former chief police inspector and political unknown, to run ostentatiously on his ticket as City Council President. Garelik's subsequent and unexpected political acts of independence (e.g., his resistance to the Mayor's special commission to investigate police corruption and his outspokenness on the dangers of urban guerrilla organizations) make it clear that he had higher political ambitions. Indeed, in 1973, Garelik put in an unsuccessful bid for Mayor in the Democratic primary along with another former police officer by the name of Mario Biaggi.

Not only are new types making claim to the leading offices of cities like New York and Philadelphia, but the political structure of such places have taken on new dimensions as well. As the old party machines continue to decline and disappear, we observed how the police bureaucracies have come to assume special significance in their new role of providing support to law-enforcer candidates and law-enforcement issues. Spurred on by a pervading popular anxiety over radicalism, student demonstrations, and Black Power, they appear to be performing many of the functions that parties served in the past. Where law permits, and sometimes in spite of the law, policemen's associations have been raising campaign funds, placing political advertisements, endorsing candidates, and organizing voters during elections.

Standing in stanch contrast to all of this is the old prereform machine model of Chicago. As some observers have testified, Chicago remains "governable" while other places like New York appear to be undergoing political deterioration. Here, neither the police nor other public employee organizations challenge the mayor; and until very recently, the nation's second largest city has stood almost alone in avoiding large scale work stoppages and law and order campaigns. In light of this, it can be argued that here, at least, is the kind of organizational control by which the many diverse parts of the city can be held together.

Included in its scope of influence are organized labor and the downtown business community. In exchange for noninterference in party matters, Daley gives support for their particular objectives. Labor union leaders, many of whom have known Daley since boyhood, are given high city construction wage rates and appointments to ranking boards and commissions. The Republican based commercial and banking interests take heart in Daley's large scale downtown urban renewal projects and expressways, activities which have restored confidence in the city's economic base. Even the "good government" reformers have found little complaint with the efficient delivery of municipal services and balanced city budgets.

Consequently, a Chicago police force which is abusive of the rights of others (as we noted earlier, this accusation was made by the Walker Report to the National Commission on the Causes and Prevention of Violence) must still answer to the Mayor. This contrasts with both New York and Philadelphia where the police and their spokesmen have come to assume a political vitality of their own. But our data also show that Chicago is by far the most violent of the three cities studied. Again and again, formal governmental control has required the active assistance of federal troops and the Illinois national guard, in addition to the city police. Simmering community tensions has made Chicago a repressive city, and for the most part, the black community has been on the receiving end.

Underlying this condition is the fact that the machine has not been sufficiently adaptable to changing conditions. As the symbol of old style ethnic power, Daley has served longer than any other mayor in Chicago history. In 1971, he was elected to his fifth four-year term with 70 percent of the popular vote. Daley's "law and order" stance informs the blacks and other dissidents that they cannot take part in the political system unless they accept the traditional machine rules of the game.

In the forward to the second edition of Harold Gosnell's classic study *Machine Politics, Chicago Model,* Theodore Lowi clarifies the impact of reform on the party organizations of America's big cities.[34] His thesis is that the disintegration of the machine did not eliminate the organizational necessities of political power; rather, it simply altered the ways and means of getting it. More precisely, Lowi contends that the reform movement has been responsible for the "replacement of Old Machines with New Machines. The bureaucracies—that is, the professionally organized, autonomous career agencies—are the New Machines."[35] He continues:

> The modern city is now well run but ungoverned because it now comprises islands of functional power before which the modern mayor stands impoverished. No mayor of a modern city has predictable means of determining whether the bosses of the New Machines—the bureau chiefs and the career commissioners—will be loyal to anything but their agency, its work, and related professional norms.[36]

Having identified the key participants and assessed their behavior in the police jurisdictions of New York, Chicago, and Philadelphia, we can now pose three models of police politics. The broad outlines as based on our observations from 1966 to 1969 are as follows:

Model 1. *New York City: Mayor-Police War:* Through legal suits, referendum battles and lobbying, the organized police bureaucracy shows considerable success in opposing the Mayor. Overall, the Mayor and the Police Commissioner remain in control though at any time their authority in police affairs could evaporate. Where the Police Commissioner is unwilling or unable to fulfill the role of the "mayor's cop," he is expected to leave. No one of the contending forces appears to be able to overawe the other. The battle rages on.

Model 2. *Philadelphia: Police Cooptation of the Mayor:* The Mayor supports the Police Commissioner and the police in virtually every issue, irrespective of the opposition. The Mayor himself has limited power resources: he is a lame duck with a disintegrating party organization. The initiative on police matters has shifted to the Police Commissioner in his role as a "cop's cop." With the close support of the local policemen's association, and with the acquiescence of the Mayor, the Commissioner has been able to assert influence beyond the police policy area.

Model 3. *Chicago: the Mayor Ascendant:* Because of the strength of the Democratic party organization as headed by the Mayor, the police are effectively limited in what they can do. The Mayor has the initiative and sets the tone on matters of police policy. At the same time, the police rely on him for support and protection. The Police Superintendent is only as successful as he has support from the Mayor which structures his role as the "mayor's cop."

NOTES

1. Under this system, selected police officers would cruise from post to post checking on the whereabouts of patrolmen.
2. *The New York Times,* March 4, 1956, Sec. VI, p. 17.
3. *Ibid.,* October 26, 1960.
4. *Ibid.,* October 27, 1960.
5. *Ibid.,* November 30, 1969.
6. James Priest Gifford, *The Political Relations of the Patrolmen's Benevolent Association (1946-1969),* (unpublished Ph.D. dissertation, Columbia University, 1970), p. 189.
7. *Ibid.,* p. 189.
8. Thomas R. Brooks, " 'No!' Says the P.B.A.," *The New York Times Magazine,* October 16, 1966, p. 37.
9. *Ibid.,* p. 126.
10. *Ibid.,* pp. 126, 128.
11. *Ibid.,* p. 128.
12. *The New York Times,* November 10, 1966.
13. Edward T. Rogowsky, Louis H. Gold, and David W. Abbott, "Police: The Civilian Review Board Controversy," in *Race and Politics in New York City* edited by Jewel Bellush and Stephen M. David (New York: Praeger Publishers, 1971), p. 92.
14. *The New York Times,* March 28, 1969.
15. *Ibid.*
16. *The New York Times,* June 19, 1969.
17. *Ibid.*
18. *The Philadelphia Inquirer,* March 12, 1967.
19. *Ibid.,* May 17, 1967.
20. *Ibid.*
21. Alexander Morisey, "The Philadelphia Police Advisory Board," unpublished Master's essay, Fels Institute, University of Pennsylvania, 1967, p. 11.
22. *The Philadelphia Evening Bulletin,* March 10, 1964.
23. *The New York Times,* August 2, 1964, Sec. VI, p. 46.
24. William Turner, *The Police Establishment* (New York: Putnam, 1968), p. 214.
25. See Lenora E. Berson, "The Toughest Cop in America Campaigns for Mayor of Philadelphia," *The New York Times Magazine,* May 16, 1971, p. 64.
26. Harold F. Gosnell, *Machine Politics, Chicago Model,* (Chicago: The University of Chicago Press, Second edition, 1968), p. vii.
27. William Turner, *op. cit.,* pp. 109, 110.
28. See *Police and Public, op. cit.*
29. See Robert H. Salisbury, "Urban Politics: The New Convergence of Power," *The Journal of Politics,* 26 (November, 1964), pp. 775-97. Also,

Edward C. Banfield and James Q. Wilson, *City Politics* (Cambridge, Mass.: Harvard University Press and M.I.T. Press, 1963), pp. 329–46.

30. "Machine Politics–Old and New," *The Public Interest* (Fall, 1967), pp. 83–92.

31. The opinion surveys primarily relied on have been reported by Angus Campbell and Howard Schuman, "Racial Attitudes in Fifteen Cities," *Supplemental Studies for the National Advisory Commission on Civil Disorders,* (New York: Praeger Edition, 1968); also *White Attitudes Toward Black People* by Angus Campbell (Ann Arbor: Institute for Social Research, The University of Michigan, 1971).

32. National Commission on the Causes and Prevention of Violence, *To Establish Justice, To Insure Domestic Tranquility* (New York: Bantam Books, 1970), p. 18.

33. *Ibid.*, pp. 38, 39.

34. See the forward to the second edition, Gosnell, *Machine Politics, Chicago Model,* op. cit.

35. *Ibid.*, p. x.

36. *Ibid.*, pp. xi, xii.

Epilogue

Much has happened since data was gathered for this study covering the period 1966 to 1969. Thus, it is tempting to expand on the material already presented. A recounting of the major events since 1969 would convey a broader perspective of political trends in each of our three sample cites. Of related interest is the opportunity this affords to test the utility of our three models of police politics, and particularly the extent to which such models provide a predictive base on which to make reliable projections.

New York City

In the years since 1969, the "war" between Mayor Lindsay and other key participants in the police establishment reached a new peak. The source of tension was persisting allegations of police corruption. Most significant was a *New York Times* survey in the Spring of 1970 which reported that millions of dollars in police graft were being collected annually. Consequently, though he was by no means directly implicated, Police Commissioner Howard Leary felt compelled to resign in the Fall of 1970.

In the face of a new investigation into police affairs, Lindsay brought Detroit's Commissioner Patrick V. Murphy to New York to succeed Leary. Murphy immediately began instituting new procedures of internal command. He increased the authority of individual precinct commanders while at the same time holding them accountable for the actions of their men. He also created a new agency, the Criminal Justice Bureau, to examine the many grey areas of criminal justice administration. More controversial was Murphy's cooperation with the Knapp Commission, a citizens group that was established by Mayor Lindsay to investigate police corruption.

More than any other single event in recent times the Knapp Commission has had a profound effect on the police jurisdiction. Headed by Whitman

Knapp, a Wall Street Lawyer, the five-man investigatory body came into being as a result of the New York Times report on police corruption. Surmounting resistance from police organizations (on separate occasions the Patrolmen's Benevolent Association and the Sergeant's Benevolent Association filed unsuccessful law suits to impede it) the Commission conducted a two-year inquiry. In public hearings, a parade of witnesses reported a wide array of corrupt police practices—everything from taking bribes to dope traffickers to shaking-down construction firms. It was also revealed how ranking police officers and city officials, including a close aide to the Mayor, were reluctant to take action even when confronted with incriminating evidence.

In a report issued August 1972, the Knapp Commission charged that corruption was indeed "widespread" and noted that neither the public nor the honest cop could trust local prosecutors to cope with the problem. Accordingly, it recommended an independent, new agency to prosecute as well as investigate "all crimes involving corruption in the criminal process." [1] In addition to other specific proposals, the Knapp report also made the following general observation: that within the Police Department, a "mixture of hostility and pride has created what the Commission has found to be the most serious roadblock to a rational attack upon police corruption: a stubborn refusal at all levels of the department to acknowledge that a serious problem exists." [2]

In light of the Commission's achievements, some observers have begun to sense a growing interest in law enforcement from various groups that could begin to turn the tide. For example, it was the Federal Law Enforcement Assistance Administration that provided the Knapp Commission with half of its financing. In 1972, the New York City Rand Institute hired the former Chief of Inspectional Services in the City Police Department to consider, among other things, how corruption could be prevented. In addition, The Fund for the City of New York took on the responsibility of analyzing the problem of how best to legalize the numbers game, a major source of entrapment of policemen. Perhaps most important, Governor Rockefeller created the office of special prosecutor to root out corruption in New York City's criminal justice system.

Whether these new forces will significantly reduce police corruption and make policemen more accountable will not be known for many years. In the meanwhile, Commissioner Patrick Murphy indicated he had had enough. After two and one-half years on the job, he announced in the Spring of 1973 that he was leaving to become head of the Police Foundation, a research group in Washington, D.C.

Philadelphia
Since he was elected as a Democrat in 1971, Mayor Frank Rizzo has violated just about all the cardinal rules of traditional partisan politics. During

the Presidential election campaign of 1972, he endorsed the Republican national candidate Richard Nixon. Then he had a falling-out with his old mentor James H. Tate and just about every other ranking Democrat in Philadelphia. He has also exchanged insults over budgeting matters with the Democratic Governor of Pennsylvania, Milton J. Shapp, and has pledged that he will work to ensure that Mr. Shapp is a "one-term Governor."

While Mayor Rizzo has not turned Philadelphia into a police state as some of his critics were predicting, he continues to think and act like a law officer. Under Rizzo, the police play a more prominent role than ever before. He has reintroduced mounted patrols to the downtown section of the city and has expanded the number of patrolmen with attack dogs riding the subways. More controversial was the arrest of dozens of anti-Nixon demonstrators—without any charges—during a campaign visit by the President in October, 1972.

Also controversial is the way the Mayor uses the Philadelphia Police Department for political purposes. In the Winter of 1972, he disclosed that he had asked the police to file reports on how each of the city's judges disposed of each criminal case handled, along with the number of times the defendant had been tried before. The information is being fed into a computer, he said, and he will make it public before the judges come up for reelection. His stated objective is to defeat those he feels have been too lenient with criminal repeaters.

Some political opponents of Rizzo have alleged that he is having their telephones tapped. Two of his accusers are former Mayors James Tate and Richardson Dilworth. Rizzo denies it and a grand jury has since cleared him of these charges. In the Summer of 1973, Philadelphia's two major newspapers accused Rizzo of employing a special thirty-three member squad of city police to spy on and harass his political enemies. Meanwhile blacks in the city remain alienated. Not only is there a scarcity of blacks in City Hall, but they resent his resistance to a Federal court ruling that he hire more black policemen.

In the face of pending investigations of the Philadelphia Police Department by the State Crime Commission and the United States Justice Department, Mayor Rizzo remains strongly protective of his former colleagues. Based on an eighteen-month study, the Pennsylvania Advisory Committee to the United States Civil Rights Commission concluded that the Department had become "a closed system in terms of responsibility and accountability." It called for a Justice Department investigation of alleged brutality, defects in complaint handling, "excessive use of arrests and failure to provide adequate protection to minority communities." [3]

Whether Frank Rizzo can make Philadelphia city government work is still very much of an open question. While he is deeply involved in politics and has political ambitions, witnesses testify that there are few professional politicians he cares for or enjoys spending time with. His solution to the problems of the city schools was to fire Superintendent Mark Shedd. He also put his own man in as President of the School Board. But that didn't avert the longest strike in the history of the schools, nor has it solved a financial crisis which threatens to close them.

Even the crime problem has failed to respond to the ministration of this law-and-order administration. During the first nine months of 1972, serious crimes have decreased in places like New York by 16.7 percent, in San Francisco by 19.4 percent, and in Washington by 26 percent. This compares to a decrease of only 1.2 percent in Philadelphia. And despite a campaign promise by Mayor Rizzo, Philadelphia is still considered by some experts to have the worst gang problem of any major United States city. Membership in the city's 105 gangs is increasing, and the total of forty gang slayings in 1972, Rizzo's first year as Mayor, fell three short of the previous year's total.

Chicago

Since 1969, the Democratic machine under Daley's leadership continues to survive. But in some important respects, pressure from outside forces are greater than ever. In the elections of November, 1972, the last of the big-city bosses suffered the heaviest setback of his political career. The voters of Cook County turned out Democratic State's Attorney (i.e., county prosecutor) Edward Hanrahan in favor of Republican challenger Bernard Carey and voted in an antimachine Democrat, Daniel Walker, as Governor. Both Hanrahan and Walker had been previously involved in weighty issues of police politics. The former was implicated in the Black Panther raid of 1969 in which Fred Hampton was killed, and the latter was responsible for "The Walker Report" which was critical of the police during the violent confrontations of the 1968 Democratic National Convention.

Carey's victory was assured by a large defection of Chicago's black voters, whom the Daley machine had always taken for granted. They were angry at Hanrahan's law and order rhetoric and the part he played in the Black Panther raid. With Hanrahan gone, Daley faces a new threat from Republicans who now control the top three prosecutors' jobs in the state: in addition to the State's Attorney position, this includes the United States Attorney's office and the Illinois State Attorney General. In the Spring of 1973, Mayor Daley's closest political associate, Alderman Thomas E. Keane, was indicted by the county grand jury on charges of conflict of interest, official misconduct and conspiracy. In addition, Federal Appellate Court Judge Otto Kerner, a former Illinois Governor, was convicted for taking bribes by a federal judge and Court Clerk Edward J. Barrett was convicted by a federal jury for getting kickbacks on voting machines.

Another threat to the Democratic organization stems from growing complaints against the Police Department. Rallied by Congressman Ralph H. Metcalfe, himself a product of the Daley machine, black leaders are demanding Superintendent Conlisk's resignation. They argue that upward spiraling violence between police and blacks must be stopped; and they want a police review board to probe complaints of police abuse. Mayor Daley has so far refused to concede on such matters.

What is perhaps just as ominous to Daley's organization are signs of growing independence by Chicago's policemen. In the Fall of 1972, they instituted a traffic-ticket writing spree in support of demands for collective bargaining. At the same time, the Confederation of Police and the Chicago Patrolmen's Association submitted a list of twenty demands to City Hall. Besides a collective bargaining agreement, they want an end to the polygraph examination requirement for a policeman who is accused of wrongdoing. They also disapprove of a rule stating that a policeman cannot plead possible self-incrimination and refuse to testify.

All told, then, the days when Richard Daley ruled his fiefdom with unquestioned authority have passed. Less certain is when it will go the way of other big cities with all that this represents in the form of bureaucratic politics.

NOTES

1. Commission to Investigate Allegations of Police Corruption and the City's Anti-Corruption Procedures, *Commission Report,* August 3, 1972, p. 15.
2. *Ibid.,* p. 6.
3. *The Philadelphia Inquirer,* August 18, 1972.

Appendix A

Decision-Making Cases in New York City, 1966-1969

CIVIL REVIEW AND ACCOUNTABILITY OF POLICE

Civil review:
1. The Law Enforcement Task Force Report.
2. The Vera Foundation study on police methods.
3. Hearings and report from the New York State Joint Legislative Committee on Election Laws and the New York State Joint Legislative Committee on Corporation Laws.
4. The International Chiefs of Police Report.
5. The New York District Attorney's investigation of police corruption.
6. The Bronx District Attorney's investigation of police corruption.
7. The Rand Corporation study of police operations.
8. Hearings by the New York State Joint Legislative Committee on Crime.
9. The Brooklyn Bar Association survey on political interference with the police.
10. The Brooklyn grand jury investigation into an attack by off-duty police on Black Panthers.
11. The New York American Civil Liberties Union study of police practices.
12. Investigations by the City Controller and the City Corporation Counsel into the Patrolmen's Benevolent Association's health and welfare fund.

Civil accountability:
1. The Civilian Review Board Controversy.
2. The appointment of the Police Commissioner.
3. Controversy over the role of the Mayor's aids during public demonstrations.
4. The PBA's attempt to issue new guidelines for the police on enforcing the law.

5. The Brooklyn Bar Association's request for an investigation of political interference with the police in civil disorders.

THE LAW AND ORDER ISSUE

1. The role of the Legal Aid Society in providing legal assistance for indigents.
2. A proposal for a new arraignment plan.
3. Proposed easing criminal standards to enhance police recruitment of minorities.
4. Controversy over the role of the Mayor's aides during public demonstrations.
5. Proposed project to provide free legal assistance in certain kinds of criminal cases.
6. The role of the Committee on Administration of Criminal Justice under Emergency Conditions.
7. Proposed emergency powers for the Mayor during civil disturbances.
8. The attempted ouster of Criminal Judge Furey.
9. Proposed guidelines on preventing unlawful police actions with regard to the Black Panthers.
10. Immunity from prosecution ruling.
11. The PBA's "get tough" guidelines.

POLICE AND COMMUNITY

1. Controversy over police membership in the John Birch Society.
2. Creation of PACT (Police and Citizens Together) to strength police–community ties.
3. Creation of the Criminal Justice Coordinating Council.
4. Creation of the Committee on Administration of Criminal Justice under Emergency Conditions.
5. Proposed easing criminal standards to encourage police recruitment of minorities.
6. Proposal to permit the police to hold outside jobs.
7. The use of grammar questions on civil service examinations for promotion of police.
8. Instituting a Preventive Enforcement Patrol program in Harlem.
9. Proposed Police Cadet program to recruit minorities.
10. Special recruiting drive to attract minorities into the police.
11. Police training program for the disadvantaged financed by the Morgan Guaranty Trust Company.

Appendix B

Decision–Making Cases in Philadelphia, 1966–1969

CIVIL REVIEW AND ACCOUNTABILITY OF POLICE

Civil review:
1. Federal grand jury investigation of police collusion with gambling ring.
2. Pennsylvania Joint Legislative Committee Investigating Narcotics views police role.
3. Staff study of police prepared for the President's Commission on Law Enforcement and Administration of Justice.
4. Three-man city committee inquiry into charges of police brutality in the schools.
5. Americans for Democratic Action's "State of the City Report."
6. Franklin Institute study on police manpower requirements.
7. Franklin Institute study comparing Philadelphia's police with police in other cities.
8. Philadelphia Human Relations Commission report on police-community relations.

Civil accountability:
1. The Police Advisory Board Controversy.
2. Appointment of the Police Commissioner.
3. Community Legal Services suit to remove the Police Commissioner.

THE LAW AND ORDER ISSUE

1. Proposal to end continuances of trials.
2. Controversy over establishing Community Legal Services, Inc.

111

3. Restricting the speech of the head of the Philadelphia chapter of the NAACP.
4. Proposals to place the city in a state of "limited emergency."
5. Providing emergency powers for the Mayor during civil disturbances.
6. Controversy over the handling of student demonstrations by the police.
7. Proposal to acquire riot-control vehicles.
8. The Philadelphia Law Enforcement Planning Council's guidelines for lawful demonstrations.
9. Proposed ban on the open display in streets or meetings of any weapon with a cutting edge.
10. The Defender Association controversy.
11. Restricting an antiwar rally.
12. Proposed ban on the carrying of weapons in colleges and universities.
13. Controlling juvenile gangs and criminal repeaters.

POLICE AND COMMUNITY

1. The North Philadelphia Congress project.
2. The Philadelphia General Hospital controversy.
3. Establishing the Philadelphia Law Enforcement Planning Council.
4. Controversy between the police and the Board of Education on law-enforcement in the schools.
5. Establishing police–community workshops.
6. Establishing a committee to coordinate emergency services during disorders.
7. Permitting police examinations in the Spanish language.
8. Proposal permitting police to enter colleges and universities unasked on evidence of persons bearing arms.
9. Police–community relations program sponsored by the Human Relations Commission.
10. The United Fund controversy.
11. Proposals to control juvenile gangs.

Appendix C

Decision-Making Cases in Chicago, 1966-1969

CIVIL REVIEW AND ACCOUNTABILITY OF POLICE

Civil review:

1. Citizens committee study called "Police and Public, A Critique and a Program."
2. The Chicago Bar Association report on police brutality.
3. The Cook County grand jury investigation into police tire-theft operations.
4. Nine-member city committee investigation of the Chicago riots of April, 1968.
5. Hearings by the Illinois Advisory Committee of the U.S. Commission on Civil Rights.
6. U.S. Justice Department financed study on police and the slums.
7. The Walker Report to the National Commission on the Causes and Prevention of Violence—"Rights in Conflict."
8. City of Chicago Report on the Democratic Convention Disturbances—"The Strategy of Confrontation."
9. U.S. grand jury investigation of the Democratic Convention disturbances.
10. Cook County Coroner's jury investigation of a police raid on the Black Panthers.
11. U.S. grand jury investigation of a police raid on the Black Panthers.
12. The American Civil Liberties Union Report—"Dissent and Disorder."

Civil accountability:

1. Establishing a registrar of complaints against the police.
2. A proposal for an inquiry into charges of favoritism in police civil service promotions.
3. The appointment of the Police Superintendent.

4. A proposed investigation of charges of police harassment of the President of the Afro-American Patrolmen's League.

THE LAW AND ORDER ISSUE

1. Establishing a police suspect file.
2. Authorizing the police to "stop and frisk."
3. Proposed emergency ban on civil rights demonstrations.
4. Legal suits against ordinances governing disorderly conduct and proposed new provisions for regulating disorderly conduct.
5. Calling out the National Guard and federal troops during civil disturbances.
6. Establishing and effecting emergency powers to deal with civil disturbances.
7. Legal suit to restrain Chicago police from interfering with news gathering.
8. Legal suit challenging police search warrant procedures.
9. Proposed use of black police in black neighborhoods during civil disorder.
10. Establishing police-security guidelines in the public schools.
11. Proposed curfew on whites in black neighborhoods.

POLICE AND COMMUNITY

1. Establishing a program to educate the police in the Spanish culture and language.
2. Controversy over police membership in the Ku Klux Klan.
3. Setting up District Community Service Sergeants in police districts.
4. The Blackstone Rangers controversy.
5. Proposal to end the police gang intelligence unit.
6. Proposing School Board cooperation with law enforcement agencies.

Index

115

About the Author

Leonard Ruchelman is Associate Professor Government at Lehigh University and is also the Director of the Urban Studies Program. He received his B.A. from Brooklyn College and his Ph.D. from Columbia University where he was a fellow in the New York Metropolitan Region Program. Dr. Ruchelman has taught at West Virginia University and Alfred University. In addition to numerous scholarly articles, he has published three other major works, *Political Careers: Recruitment Through the Legislature, Big City Mayors,* and *Who Rules the Police?*